WITTGENSTEIN'S RELIGIOUS POINT OF VIEW

Continuum Studies in British Philosophy:

WITTGENSTEIN'S RELIGIOUS POINT OF VIEW

Tim Labron

continuum
LONDON • NEW YORK

Continuum International Publishing Group
The Tower Building
11 York Road
London
SE1 7NX

80 Maiden Lane
Suite 704
New York, NY 10038

British Library Cataloguing-in-Publication Data
A catalogue record for this book is available from the British Library.

ISBN: 0-8264-9027-1 (hardback)

Library of Congress Cataloging-in-Publication Data
A catalog record for this book is available from the Library of Congress.

Typeset by Fakenham Photosetting Limited, Fakenham, Norfolk
Printed and bound in Great Britain by Biddles Ltd, King's Lynn, Norfolk

Contents

Contents

Introduction

Wittgenstein once remarked to his friend M. O'C. Drury, 'I am not a religious man but I cannot help seeing every problem from a religious point of view.'[1] This reference, in particular, has fuelled attempts to determine the exact nature of the relation between Wittgenstein's philosophy and his personal attitude towards religious belief. The debate ranges from saying that Wittgenstein and his philosophy are straightforwardly religious, to saying that religion plays no part either in his philosophy or in his life more generally. Rather than trying to argue whether or not Wittgenstein and his philosophy can be said to be religious, this study is primarily focused on issues in the philosophy of language, and intended to demonstrate that there is, indeed, an interesting and fruitful analogy between Wittgenstein's later philosophy and a 'religious point of view' which he himself once described as 'Hebraic'.

But can Wittgenstein's views on philosophy be plausibly discussed in terms of analogies at all? As he himself notes, the use of a simile or analogy is helpful: ' "It's all excellent similes", he said in a lecture of Freud's work, and of his own contribution to philosophy. "What I invent are new *similes*." '[2] And 'a good simile refreshes the intellect'.[3] Moreover, Rush Rhees notes the comparison of Wittgenstein's method and psychoanalysis: 'He sometimes spoke of analogies in *method*. The functional disorders which philosophy treats appear as delusions and dreams of our language.'[4] In what follows, I shall argue that, consistently with Wittgenstein's more general remarks about the illuminating power of a good simile or carefully chosen analogy, the distinctive character of his own conception of philosophy is thrown into relief by a specifically *religious* analogy. In particular, Hebraic thought provides an interesting analogy to illuminate the distinct nature of Wittgenstein's later philosophy.

Before arriving at Hebraic thought as a viable analogy for Wittgenstein's 'religious point of view' and his later thought, it is helpful to address his early thought. Indeed, Wittgenstein writes in the Preface to the

Philosophical Investigations: 'It suddenly seemed to me that I should publish those old thoughts and the new ones together: that the latter could be seen in the right light only by contrast with and against the background of my old way of thinking.'[5] Wittgenstein's 'old thoughts', as found in the *Tractatus Logico-Philosophicus*,[6] will be discussed in the first chapter in order to better understand his 'new ones'.

The first chapter will also address Phillip Shields's attempt to understand Wittgenstein's 'religious point of view' since his interpretation – as found in his work *Logic and Sin in the Writings of Ludwig Wittgenstein* – will be shown to be largely based on Wittgenstein's early thought.[7] Shields's project places the corpus of Wittgenstein's works largely within a Tractarian framework whereby logical form requires language to connect to elements of reality (simple objects) to ensure meaning and avoid philosophical confusion. Shields not only reduces Wittgenstein's philosophy to his early thought, he also confounds it with religion. He will be shown to associate logical form and a rule-governed language with God, and philosophical confusion with sin. In short: Shields misses the unique character of Wittgenstein's later thought, wrongly identifies Wittgenstein's philosophy as religious, and consequently misconstrues Wittgenstein's philosophy and his 'religious point of view'.

Despite Shields's problematic conception of Wittgenstein's philosophy and 'religious point of view' it is useful to discuss his work, not only because it is a helpful contrast to Norman Malcolm's discussion,[8] but also because it has been influential in contemporary discussions of Wittgenstein and his 'religious point of view'.[9] This study agrees that Shields's work, despite its problems, should be addressed in the discussion of Wittgenstein and his 'religious point of view'. Shields offers a striking example of how a problematic construal of Wittgenstein's conception of philosophy and serious confusions about the relation between philosophy and religious belief more generally, combine into an interpretative model that hinders, rather than advances, our understanding of Wittgenstein's work.

In contrast to Shields's project, the distinction between Wittgenstein's early and later philosophy will be highlighted. Indeed, it will be shown that Wittgenstein's later understanding of language, and his conception of the role of philosophy, necessitate a study of Wittgenstein's 'religious point of view' that is dramatically different from Shields's. Wittgenstein's philosophy turns from an analysis of an underlying logical syntax that is thought to be the base of language, to the description of the application of language in the form of life. Moreover, Wittgenstein's later understanding of the seriousness and depth of philosophical confusion is also an important aspect of the 'therapeutic' nature of his later philosophy. An understanding of the above aspects of Wittgenstein's later thought is essential since it is the base from which an analogical comparison will be made with a 'religious point of view', and Hebraic thought in particular.

The second chapter will discuss Malcolm's conception of Wittgenstein's philosophy and a 'religious point of view'.[10] Malcolm, in contrast to Shields, clearly differentiates Wittgenstein's Tractarian thought from his later conception of language, and centres a 'religious point of view' on the latter. Malcolm argues, for example, that Wittgenstein's later conception of language moves away from theories and explanations for meaning. He takes note of Wittgenstein's remark that 'you make a study of a particular language-game. Then you can say to someone: "Look at it! That's how it is! Don't ask why, but take it as a fact, without explanation!" '[11] Malcolm then observes the similarity between this aspect of Wittgenstein's later thought and a 'religious point of view': 'It is God's will' has a 'logical force similar to "That's how it is!" Both expressions tell us to stop asking "Why?" and instead accept a fact!'[12] Malcolm will be shown to discern interesting similarities between Wittgenstein's later philosophy and a 'religious point of view'.

Malcolm's discussion of the analogical nature of Wittgenstein's later thought and a 'religious point of view' is also helpful in so far as it recognizes the distinction between philosophy and religion. In contrast to Shields, Malcolm builds his discussion on Wittgenstein's later philosophy and only uses religious themes to show interesting similarities between the two. Consequently, Malcolm provides meaningful groundwork that invites further discussion of Wittgenstein and a 'religious point of view' by showing the distinct natures of Wittgenstein's early and later thought, and how the latter, in particular, is *analogical* to a 'religious point of view'.

The third chapter will continue to discuss the distinct natures of Wittgenstein's early and later thought by contrasting Greek thought and Hebraic thought respectively. Wittgenstein, for instance, remarked to his friend M. O'C. Drury in conversation:

Of course it [Origen's idea][13] was rejected. It would make nonsense of everything else. If what we do now is to make no difference in the end, then all the seriousness of life is done away with. Your religious ideas have always seemed to me more Greek than biblical. Whereas my thoughts are one hundred percent Hebraic.[14]

Wittgenstein indicates that there is a distinction between Greek and Hebraic thought, and that he disassociates his thought from Greek thought, but associates it with Hebraic thought. The aspect of Greek thought drawn upon will be based on foundational theories of language. For example, the early Wittgenstein's simple objects, Shields's pre-established conditions, and Platonic Forms, will be shown to remove significance from normative applications of language by creating additional exterior and causal connections to explain meaning. Although distinctly unique, in each of these cases there is an additional element to which language must connect, be it the Tractarian simple object or the sense of language being a representation of the ideal Forms. Once again, these types of thought are vastly different, but the point will be made within this study that each can be read, within the context of the philosophy of language, as distancing meaning and authority for language from concrete practices (i.e. from the applications of language) to external and abstract strictures to which language must adhere.

In contrast to theories that distance thought and language from the concrete and practical, and thus to theories that attempt to explain language through foundational categories, the later Wittgenstein insists on an understanding of language that is based on concrete practices. The final assurance of meaning is not based on the simple object, but on the application of language. In the light of this distinction between theories that posit additional connections for language and meaning, and Wittgenstein's later thought, the fourth chapter will show that Hebraic thought corresponds with Wittgenstein's later thought. There is a link between Wittgenstein's remarks, that he has a 'religious point of view' and that his thoughts are 'one hundred percent Hebraic'.[15]

A discussion of Semitic thought and Wittgenstein need not end in a negative correlation as is commonly accepted, but can lead to an insightful comparison. The fourth chapter will begin with a discussion of the often-assumed notion that Wittgenstein regards his Jewish background, and Jewish thought in general, as unsatisfactory.[16] On the contrary, it will be shown that he in fact associates his own thought with Jewish thought in a positive way. The long-standing notion that Wittgenstein rejects Semitic thought is questionable and needs to be seriously reconsidered.

In contrast to former discussions of Wittgenstein's 'religious point of view', this study will show that a particular strand of Hebraic thought based in the Judaic tradition (in contrast to medieval Jewish philosophy in line with Maimonides) provides an interesting analogy for Wittgenstein's later philosophy. There is a similarity between Wittgenstein's understanding of meaning in the philosophy of language and Hebraic thought's understanding of meaning within a religious context. Wittgenstein's later thought and Hebraic thought will be shown to attach meaning to the historical and contemporary applications of language – the forms of life – in contrast to positing additional elements or foundational theories beyond normative practices.[17]

The analogous nature of Wittgenstein's later thought and Hebraic thought will be shown through the example of the Israelites and the golden calf. Confusion within the philosophy of language can be said to be the result of philosophical idols (e.g. the simple object) and confusion within a religious context can also be said to be a result of idols (e.g. golden calf). Moreover, the 'treatment' for confusion and idols will be shown to be similar; that is, to turn from idols to the form of life where meaning and authority do reside. Wittgenstein's later conception of the serious problems of philosophical confusion and idols and the required 'treatment' will be shown analogically within the Hebraic context of the Israelites and the golden calf.

It is important to remember the tension that should remain in any study of Wittgenstein and religion. No attempt is made to show that Wittgenstein is, in fact, religious – let alone a Jewish believer in particular. Moreover, to simply equate his philosophy with religion only leads to confusion. It needs to be made clear what is meant by 'religious' and what is meant by 'philosophical'. In contrast to equating philosophy and religion, a particular aspect of philosophy and a particular aspect of a religious viewpoint will be discussed on an analogical basis. The key to this analogical comparison is Wittgenstein's later philosophy of language, while Hebraic thought is used to illuminate its unique character. This study will show that Hebraic thought based in the Judaic tradition is an original and valuable means to interpret the analogy between Wittgenstein's later philosophy and his 'religious point of view'.

Endnotes

1   M. O'C. Drury, 'Conversations with Wittgenstein', in *Recollections of Wittgenstein*, ed. Rush Rhees (Oxford: Oxford University Press, 1984), 79.

2   Ray Monk, *Ludwig Wittgenstein: The Duty of Genius* (London: Jonathan Cape, 1990), 357.

3   Ludwig Wittgenstein, *Culture and Value*, ed. G. H. von Wright in collaboration with Heikki Nyman, trans. Peter Winch (Chicago: University of Chicago Press, 1984), 1.

4   Rush Rhees, *Discussions of Wittgenstein*, ed. Rush Rhees (Bristol: Thoemmes Press, 1996), 45.

5   Ludwig Wittgenstein, *Philosophical Investigations*, trans. G. E. M. Anscombe (Oxford: Basil Blackwell, 1988), viii.

6   Ludwig Wittgenstein, *Tractatus Logico-Philosophicus*, trans. C. K. Ogden, with an Introduction by Bertrand Russell (London: Routledge & Kegan Paul, 1986).

7   Phillip R. Shields, *Logic and Sin in the Writings of Ludwig Wittgenstein* (Chicago: University of Chicago Press, 1993).

8   Norman Malcolm, *Wittgenstein: A Religious Point of View?*, ed. Peter Winch (New York: Cornell University Press, 1995).

9   Fergus Kerr, for example, notes that 'Shields has a good subject and a case which provokes disagreement and further refection. Of the many recent books about Wittgenstein, *Logic and Sin* is one of the very few that are well worth having.' Fergus Kerr, review of *Logic and Sin in the Writings of Ludwig Wittgenstein*, by Phillip R. Shields, in *Modern Theology*, 10 (July 1994), 301. Additionally, Eric O. Springsted writes: 'What Shields uncovered in Wittgenstein's religious sensibility is something genuine and profound ... Shields has not just written an important book on Wittgenstein but an enlightening work that invites further reflection.' Eric O. Springsted, review of *Logic and Sin in the Writings of Ludwig Wittgenstein*, by Phillip R. Shields, in *Cross Currents*, 43, 3 (Fall 1993), 413.

10 Shields and Malcolm seriously consider the relation between Wittgenstein's thought and religion, and then offer 'religious' analogies. This method, however, contrasts sharply with Brian R. Clack's approach: 'Our question ... is whether atheism is the inevitable consequence of an acceptance of Wittgenstein's approach to religious belief, and what kind of atheism that could be' (125). The answer is a 'despairing, apocalyptic atheism that arises from Wittgenstein's philosophy of religion, the frustrated and bitter recognition that the passionate beauty of the religious life is no longer open to us' (129). Moreover, 'it would ... be somewhat perplexing were someone to accept all that Wittgenstein has to say about religion in his later period and yet still be able to continue in his or her faith' (125). Brian R. Clack, *An Introduction to Wittgenstein's Philosophy of Religion* (Edinburgh: Edinburgh University Press, 1999).

11 Wittgenstein, *Philosophical Investigations*, 200. Malcolm, *Wittgenstein*, 86.

12 Malcolm, *Wittgenstein*, 86.

13 Drury states: 'Origen taught that at the end of time there would be a final restitution of all things. That even Satan and the fallen angels would be restored to their former glory.' Drury, 'Conversations with Wittgenstein', 161. Origen's idea of *apokatastasis* (re-establishment) denotes that, through time, all return to God: 'The end is always like the beginning.' Origen, *De Principiis*, in *Ante-Nicene Fathers*, ed. Alexander Roberts and James Donaldson, vol. 4 (Buffalo: Christian Literature Publishing, 1887), I, vi, 2. The implication is an ultimate return to an incorporeal existence in God in spite of all practices.

14 Drury, 'Conversations with Wittgenstein', 161.

15 *Ibid.*

16 Monk, *The Duty of Genius*, 314–17.

17 Hebraic thought will be covered in more detail in the fourth chapter. For now, let it suffice to briefly quote Solomon Schechter: God, he says, is 'mainly reached, not by metaphysical deductions, but, as was the case with the Rabbis, through personal experience of his revelation and his continuous operations in the world, [and he] cannot possibly be removed from it'. Solomon Schechter, *Aspects of Rabbinic Theology*, with an introduction by Neil Gillman and by Louis Finkelstein (Woodstock, VT: Jewish Lights Publishing, 1993),

25. In effect, Schechter is saying that we must simply look within the world itself for meaning, not to external metaphysical connections that are distanced from the world. Hebraic thought, in contrast to Greek thought, will be shown to follow Wittgenstein's remark, 'don't think, but look!' Wittgenstein, *Philosophical Investigations*, § 66.

1

Wittgenstein's Early Philosophy and a 'Religious Point of View'

The philosophy of language forms the basis of the investigation into Wittgenstein's thought and an analogical 'religious point of view'. The nature of the analogy depends on whether Wittgenstein's early or later conception of language is the focus. It is thereby helpful to discuss Wittgenstein's early conception of language as found in the *Tractatus Logico-Philosophicus*. Moreover, Wittgenstein considers his early philosophy to be a helpful background that more clearly shows the nature of his later philosophy.[1] It is important to recognize the distinct nature of Wittgenstein's later philosophy since it, in particular, is what will be shown to be analogical to a religious point of view.

Phillip R. Shields, however, focuses on the logic of the *Tractatus*. He takes Wittgenstein's remark that he cannot help seeing every problem from a religious point of view to be an obvious statement that 'being a logician has clear affinities with being religious'.[2] Shields's singular focus on Wittgenstein as a logician contrasts with the mainstream approach of using Wittgenstein's 'religious' remarks (i.e. comments on the mystical, and religion) as proof of his religious nature. It is one thing to argue, as seems most obvious, that Wittgenstein must have some connection with religion as is evident through his remarks on religion, but Shields claims that Wittgenstein's understanding of logic is evidence of the religious nature of his thought. Despite this unusual line of argument, Shields nonetheless comes to the conclusion that Wittgenstein is religious. Indeed, he claims that Wittgenstein's writings *are* religious.[3] What is unique about Shields's interpretation is that it is derived from an analysis of Wittgenstein's writings on logic, not from a preoccupation with his 'religious' remarks or comments on the mystical.

Shields prefaces his discourse with the intention to focus on Wittgenstein's philosophical and logical argumentation to show its religious nature, while avoiding unnecessary references to biographical and historical evidence.[4] This study will follow Shields's lead in this respect by focusing on methodological issues. The adaptation of such an approach is not to suggest that biographical evidence is irrelevant, only that it is worthwhile, as a methodological choice, to restrict the focus to his writings in an attempt to appreciate them in and of themselves. The details of Wittgenstein's personal life may indeed help us to understand him, but this is simply the presentation of a study of his writings and his conception of language.

Shields's intent to demonstrate an equivalence between Wittgenstein's philosophy and a 'religious point of view' does not take the shift in Wittgenstein's later thought into account and thereby leads to confusion, not clarity. Nevertheless, just as a discussion of Wittgenstein's early thought provides more insight into his later thought, a discussion of Shields's problematic project reveals the importance of clearly addressing Wittgenstein's later philosophy. It will be shown that Wittgenstein's later understanding of language and conception of philosophy are better suited than his early philosophy to discussions of an analogical religious point of view. However, the discussion will begin with Wittgenstein's early thought and Shields as a background to more clearly show the importance of acknowledging the unique character of Wittgenstein's later philosophy.

Wittgenstein's Tractarian say and show distinction

In order to show the distinction between Wittgenstein's early and later philosophy, and to demonstrate the basis of Shields's argument, it is necessary to start at the beginning, with Wittgenstein's say/show distinction. Not only is it necessary to discuss the say/show distinction in order to understand the transition in Wittgenstein's thought and the basis of Shields's method, it is also necessary to understand the *Tractatus* itself. Rush Rhees comments:

This question of the relation of logic and empirical propositions has always been one of 'the cardinal problems of philosophy'. Most forms of scepticism have centred around it, for instance. But we cannot understand it unless we are clear about what can be said and what can only be shown. This is the point of the *Tractatus*.[5]

The say/show distinction, the logic of the relation between propositions and the world, is a central concern for both Shields and Wittgenstein.[6] The emphasis is to discern what can be logically said in the world, in contrast to falling into the confusion of saying what can only be shown.

To understand the relation between logic and the proposition, that is, to understand why some things can be said while others are only shown, it is helpful to develop Wittgenstein's understanding of the relation between language and the world. What can be said is discussed by Wittgenstein through the picture theory of meaning, that language works by picturing actual or possible states of affairs in the world. An example is found, according to Wittgenstein, in hieroglyphic writing 'which pictures the facts it describes'.[7] Just as a hieroglyph pictures the world, so a proposition pictures the world, and as Wittgenstein writes, is 'a picture of reality'.[8]

Take, for example, a proposition such as 'There is a cat on my desk.' This proposition has a sense because it pictures a possible state of affairs. The structure of the proposition is thereby related to the structure of the world. We can, for example, change the construction of the proposition (or hieroglyph) and end up with an entirely different picture: 'The desk is on my cat!' The proposition and the hieroglyph must have a strict structure that conforms to the world in order for there to be a meaning that we can comprehend. Thus, a proposition pictures reality by being a logical map of a possible state of affairs, which can then be verified by comparing the picture with reality. Just as a painter can paint a picture of a castle with a tree beside it, we know that this is a possible structure and, by checking the world, we can confirm that indeed there is a castle with a tree beside it just like the one in the picture.

That a proposition can be said, and the fact that it has sense, go hand in hand – there is a link between the proposition and reality. Note, however, that the proposition above has a sense without checking the actual state of affairs to see if it is true or false, that its sense is independent of its truth or falsehood, yet it *must* be either true or false. A painter can add or subtract from a painting, but even if there are additions or subtractions to a scene, that is to say even if it is a false picture, we can still make sense of it. If a proposition is to have meaning through picturing a possible state of affairs, then it must be a logical picture that is bipolar, that is, it must by definition be true or false.[9] If a proposition is not capable of being true or false, then it is either senseless (which will be discussed later) or it is nonsense. In other words, if a proposition is to tell us something about the world, if it is to have sense, then it must express something that can be pictured in the world. We can picture a tree beside a castle, whether there is actually a tree beside it or not, but it is hard to imagine the picture and truth or falsity of 'Blue limbs are on holiday', which is not simply false, but nonsense.

Thus far, the discussion has concerned ordinary language. However, the actual relation of language to the world is, on the Tractarian view, much deeper. Propositions can be broken down into more basic building blocks, namely, elementary propositions. Indeed, complex propositions are, according to the Tractarian view, truth functions of elementary propositions (which are truth functions of themselves),[10] and are thereby determined in sense by elementary propositions that are dependent on the functions of their constituent names.[11] More specifically, propositions can be broken down into elementary propositions which are composed of names, not further propositions, and a name comes into direct contact with reality when it is linked with the world, at which point 'a name means an object. The object is its meaning.'[12] The name stands for an external object and only has meaning as tied to this external object. The name substitutes, or takes the place of, a simple object.[13]

The idea here is that complex propositions can be true or false and need to be compared to the world. If one complex proposition is true, 'My pen is red', then the complex proposition, 'My pen is blue', is false. However, elementary propositions, which are concatenations of names for simple objects, result in a different order of logic since names must name something or they have no meaning. While we still understand the meaning of 'My pen is blue', even if it is false, there are no false names that we could understand. It is in this context that Wittgenstein remarks, 'names resemble points; propositions resemble arrows, they have sense'.[14] The name is the base of the proposition and the contact with the world, while the proposition is a combination of parts that points to its sense and maintains meaning whether it is true or false.

There is, then, a move from the picture of a proposition to logically simple names, at which point the picture, *via* the name, links with reality.[15] When this connection between the structure of the picture and reality hold, that is, when the general proposition pictures a possible state of affairs and the elementary propositions which compose the general proposition are true, then they link with reality – the name has an object – and the picture is a fact. What this indicates, then, is that the general proposition has meaning in the light of its internal sense being a possible state of affairs, and that it is a possible state of affairs since a name links directly with its object yielding an external meaning. There are no further propositions; instead, there are the simple object and name.

It should be obvious now that the word 'cat', from the initial proposition 'There is a cat on my desk', is not a name of a simple object. Instead, it is part of ordinary language, which is composite and divisible through logical analysis, as Wittgenstein thought by working through to the name and simple object. Moreover, the cat can be simplified into a paw, a tail, a whisker, etc. ..., in which case the resulting proposition would describe the relation of each part of the cat and then its relation to being on my desk. Unsurprisingly, Wittgenstein never did give an example of a simple object or name due to the considerably complex and lengthy task of working through language to the underlying logical syntax. Since there is no example of a name for a simple object, it follows that there are no examples of an elementary proposition either. The simple object and elementary proposition are assumed; there is no analysis that has been completed to the end of either. Nevertheless, Wittgenstein writes: 'It does not go against our feeling, that *we* cannot analyse propositions so far to mention the elements by name; no, we feel that the world must consist of elements.'[16] The use of the word 'cat' necessarily requires, through Wittgenstein's logical syntax, the existence of elementary propositions and simple objects. The statement, 'The cat is on my desk', is simply ordinary language, while beneath this ordinary language is the logical syntax culminating in the simple object.

At this point the logical syntax of the proposition is thought to be worked out – at least in theory – with no further steps being required. The independent simple name, as the final step of working out the logical syntax, is necessary in order to get around the idea that further propositions are required to complete the analysis of the proposition to secure understanding. Wittgenstein needs the simple name to connect with the simple object in order to maintain a determined sense and to side step the problem of relativism, since if a name does not stand directly for an object, then further propositions are required entailing an infinite regress.[17]

Instead of an infinite regress of the possible facts that can be pictured, Wittgenstein posits the limit of names and objects within the world:

The world is the totality of facts, not things.

The world is determined by the facts, and by these being *all* the facts.

For the totality of facts determines both what is the case, and also all that is not the case.[18]

It then follows that 'the specification of all true elementary propositions describes the world completely',[19] and 'the totality of propositions is the language'.[20] The possible configurations of the simple objects are the boundary of language. In the *Tractatus*, facts, propositions, language, and the world, are limited to 'what is the case'. This is what can be said. It is the limit of language, beyond which there is nothing for the name to link with. Accordingly, that which is shown is beyond propositions (what can be said), and is transcendental. A proposition must be a possible state of affairs in the world, and the transcendental is obviously not a structure in the world and therefore, it is not sayable. To cross into the transcendental with names in an attempt to say that which can only be shown is to cross the limit of language into metaphysics, nonsense and confusion.

The main point is that once the two distinct forms of the say/show distinction are mingled, confusion results. There is no metalanguage that can explain language from outside the sayable. Hence, Wittgenstein writes, 'What we cannot speak about we must pass over in silence.'[21] We must respect the fundamental limits of language and not cross the limit into philosophical confusion.

Wittgenstein, however, saw that which is passed over in silence as very significant, in fact, the most significant.[22] There is a category other than that which can be said and has sense, namely, that which is shown and is senseless, but not nonsense such as 'The blue limbs are on holiday.' As has been shown, if a proposition has meaning independent of its truth or falsity (i.e. if the proposition 'There is a cat on my desk' makes sense, whether there is or is not a cat on my desk), then this shows that there is a link between language and reality due to the common structure between the proposition and the world. Propositions do represent reality, but they do not, however, explain how they represent reality;

to do so we would need to stand outside logic and the world with our propositions.[23]

Wittgenstein calls this link between propositions and reality 'logical form';[24] it cannot be said, and is thereby senseless and only shown. It is not part of the content of a proposition and cannot be stated; rather, it is the eternal form of the world and of what is logically possible. In order to see why this is the case, it must be understood that logical form is not an extra substance, in addition to propositions and the world, that binds them together with some sort of glue as if it is also something that can be said; instead, it is only shown in the common structure of propositions and the world. What is shown, then, is the fact that 'what any picture, of whatever form, must have in common with reality, in order to be able to depict it – correctly or incorrectly – in any way at all, is logical form, i.e. the form of reality'.[25] Yet once again, although the representation of facts through pictures involves two factors, the proposition and the fact, there is no third factor called logical form to be expressed by language: 'What can be shown, cannot be said.'[26] Instead of being asserted by language, logical form is shown through language.[27] As Wittgenstein states:

> Propositions cannot represent the logical form: this mirrors itself in the propositions. That which mirrors itself in language, language cannot represent. That which expresses *itself* in language, *we* cannot express by language. The propositions *show* the logical form of reality, they exhibit it.[28]

The proposition says, for example, 'The cat is on my desk', and this can be verified through checking the proposition against reality. However, the fact that there is a connection between the proposition and the world (logical form), that we can check the proposition against reality, cannot be stated, for language would need to go beyond itself in order to state this relation.

To say that logic, for instance, says nothing,[29] does not mean that it has little significance; rather, as previously stated, it enables propositions to picture reality. Moreover, the transcendental is not accidental, and it is not a possible state of affairs as propositions are; instead, if it is to be of value, it must be beyond the world, which then implies beyond the limit of language. Wittgenstein writes:

There is indeed the inexpressible. This *shows* itself; it is the mystical.[30]

The sense of the world must lie outside the world. In the world every-thing is as it is and happens as it does happen. *In* it there is no value – and if there were, it would be of no value. If there is a value which is of value, it must lie outside all happening and being-so. For all happening and being-so is accidental. It must lie outside the world.[31]

Hence, for logic to say nothing is, in fact, crediting logic with more value and significance than if it did say something. Paul Engelmann accurately discerns:

A whole generation of disciples was able to take Wittgenstein for a positivist because he has something of enormous importance in common with the positivists: he draws the line between what we can speak about and what we must be silent about just as they do. The difference is only that they have nothing to be silent about. Positivism holds – and this is its essence – that what we can speak about is all that matters in life. *Whereas Wittgenstein passionately believes that all that really matters in human life is precisely what, in his view, we must be silent about.* When he nevertheless takes immense pains to delimit the unimportant, it is not the coastline of that island which he is bent on surveying with such meticulous accuracy, but the boundary of the ocean.[32]

Wittgenstein's intent is to clarify language, but not to reject that which cannot be said as irrelevant. What cannot be said is of the utmost importance.

Within the category of the transcendental is the positive content of logic and value, including ethics, aesthetics and religion. Like logic, ethics, aesthetics and religion are shown, but cannot be said since they cannot, for instance, be reduced to a possible state of affairs and must remain independent of the measure; that is, since propositions cannot say anything more than the state of affairs,[33] they cannot speak of the transcendental. Yet, once again, even though the positive content beyond the limit cannot be said, it is shown formally in the structure of what can be said. Logical form enables propositions to be stated – true or false – and while it permeates everything that is sayable (it is the one logic of language), it says nothing itself of what is in the world (possibilities), while what can be said, as is found in, e.g. science, does speak of what is in the world. There is an *a priori* order in the world and it is a logical form that says nothing; it is independent of the empirical, yet it is necessary for anything to be said of the empirical.

A Tractarian reading of Wittgenstein's 'religious point of view'

If Wittgenstein's early philosophy is the basis for a discussion of a 'religious point of view', then the result is a project like Shields's. He maintains Wittgenstein's Tractarian logic and thereby utilizes the say/show distinction within his project. In other words, Shields's philosophy of language centres on the *Tractatus*. He states, 'it is the demand for clarity that underlies the need for the sharp say/show distinction, and it is the say/show distinction that in turn ensures the possibility of the absolute clarity of logical and grammatical form'.[34] He continually emphasizes the separation between the world and that which cannot be said, the transcendental, and carries the rigorous limit of the say/show distinction through the entire corpus of Wittgenstein's writings.

Shields does not, however, leave Wittgenstein's Tractarian logic and the say/show distinction at the level of logical analysis; instead, he imbues it with a religious significance. Indeed, Shields easily moves from a discussion of Tractarian logic to a discussion of religion as two sides of the same coin. As noted earlier, Shields claims that Wittgenstein's writings are not to be understood as having merely peripheral relevance to religion, but 'are fundamentally religious as they stand', that they 'form a particular ethical/religious view of the world'.[35] In Shields's discussion of Wittgenstein's writings, there is no cryptic suggestion of Wittgenstein's religious underpinnings or initialization of peripheral 'religious' quotes from Wittgenstein. Rather, there is a deliberate and clear-cut attempt to show that his philosophy is religious as it stands, as it is revealed in Wittgenstein's conception of logic. According to Shields, the 'seriousness' and 'religious' nature of Wittgenstein's philosophy

> indicates the centrality of an apocalyptic struggle between the disturbing spectre of confusion and degeneracy and a deeply rooted belief in the

ultimate clarity and dignity of meaning, as it were, between the forces
of darkness and the forces of light. That this struggle is simultaneously
a religious struggle and a struggle to understand logic will become
apparent.[36]

For Shields, Tractarian logic is the pivotal argument in proof of the religious
nature of Wittgenstein's philosophy, and is equated with the monumental
battle between darkness and light – confusion and clarity. More specifically, he discerns the forces of light: 'at the root of Wittgenstein's critique
of metaphysics I found ... the outline of a religious picture of the world
– a picture that is broadly Judeo-Christian, usually Augustinian and
frequently Calvinistic'.[37] The religious nature of Wittgenstein's writings,
and in particular his writings on logic, are not, for Shields, comparable to
religion; rather, Wittgenstein's writings *are* religious: 'the continuity of the
say/show distinction reflects the continuity of his [Wittgenstein's] ethical
and religious concern'.[38]

The logical framework Shields builds on to attempt to demonstrate Wittgenstein's writings as religious in nature, and in particular
Calvinistic, is Wittgenstein's distinction between what can be said and
what cannot be said but only shown. This boundary is the limit that
cannot be crossed, and in Shields's hands it is the limit that separates the
darkness of philosophical confusion from the bright clarity of Tractarian
logic, the frontline of the struggle between meaning and confusion. We
stand on the side of what can be said, and in so doing remain in the light,
but if we attempt to cross over to the other side, across the demarcation of
what can be said into the realm of what can only be shown, we can only
fall into confusion.

The religious significance of the shown resides, for Shields, in God as
compared to logical form since 'the ultimacy of logical form shows us
something of what it would mean to speak of the sovereignty and glory
of God'.[39] The impetus to compare or relate logical form with God is not
entirely incomprehensible. Common conceptions of God, and certainly
Shields's conception of God, do share certain characteristics, particularly the non-contingent and the transcendental. It is important to note
that although Shields is saying Wittgenstein's writings *are* religious, he is
not saying logical form *is* God. Yet God and logical form are intimately
related in Shields's work; indeed, he regards Wittgenstein's writings on

logic to demonstrate God, and he emphasizes this correlation with a Reformed (Calvinistic) understanding:

> Wittgenstein's characterization of God bears an illuminating resemblance to the transcendent Deity represented in the Reformed tradition [in the] sense of the powerful Other, of that on which all things ultimately depend, to which all are ultimately related, which both limits and sustains human activities.[40]

It is interesting to note that Wittgenstein never explicitly characterizes God, yet Shields draws the opposite conclusion. Wittgenstein's Tractarian logic and Reformed theology are, for Shields, simply different ways of describing the foundation of reality as shown – God and logical form. The reason Shields makes this claim is that, for him, God and logical form are closely related, so when Wittgenstein discusses logic he is, *ipso facto*, discussing aspects of God's will.[41]

Once logical form is associated with God, it is not surprising that what we are giving assent to is not just a logical grammar, according to Shields, but God's will. He states,

> for Wittgenstein, the possibility that language has a clear sense is dependent on our acceptance of a preexisting horizon. The acceptance of logical or grammatical form must be deeper than a mere verbal assent. What we accept will never yield complete clarity unless it stands fast by becoming the unquestioned ground for what we do in our lives. In this sense, what is required of us is absolute, and this is what it means for Wittgenstein to speak of doing the will of God.[42]

Shields posits the absolute, the determined sense of logical form that must be accepted, and if accepted one is doing God's will. Thus, as Shields writes, a 'logical, or grammatical form, stands over us like the will of God, both limiting and sustaining us, and ... what is required of us is to be fully reconciled to it'.[43] Logical form, like the will of God, limits what can be said, stands against philosophical confusion, and sustains the ability to be able to say something.

The stipulation of God's will to enable what we can say, and limit what we cannot say, is integral to Shields's theory since 'without God, understood in the sense of a binding horizon, expressions would mean whatever anyone wanted them to mean, and each interpretation would be neither better nor worse than another'.[44] The use of God to secure a theory is not an original idea. Descartes, for example, writes:

> I plainly see that the certainty and truth of all knowledge depends uniquely on my knowledge of the true God, to such an extent that I was incapable of perfect knowledge about anything else until I knew him. And now it is possible for me to achieve full and certain knowledge of countless matters, both concerning God himself and other things whose nature is intellectual, and also concerning the whole of that corporeal nature which is the subject of pure mathematics.[45]

Thus Shields, like Descartes, assumes meaning would be indeterminate if it were not for God. In other words, God secures knowledge. Likewise, the base of Wittgenstein's Tractarian logic entails that simple names attach directly to objects to counter an infinite regress.[46] Wittgenstein states, 'It does not go against our feeling, that *we* cannot analyse propositions so far to mention the elements by name; no, we feel that the world must consist of elements.'[47] Shields similarly posits the idea that there must be some anchor to fix logic and meaning, namely the pre-established conditions, or God. Shields writes, 'determinations of logical form, or logical grammar, are utterly dependent on preestablished conditions ... in terms of the internal form of tractarian objects'.[48] The early Wittgenstein thought an infinite regress would result if there were no simple object, while Shields thinks the door to relativism will be opened if there are no God-given or, as it were, pre-established conditions. In both cases there is an assumed final anchor point – God's pre-established conditions or the simple object. Wittgenstein, however, posited simples, not God. Even so, Shields attaches the idea of God's will to the Tractarian logic to remove doubt from the certainty of his method.

In Shields's writing logical form and God's will are given as the *a priori* buttresses that enable and limit what can be said. The limit surrounding what can be said is, in the light of the association with God's will, suffused with ethical considerations. As Shields says, 'once the dictates of logical grammar are compared to the will of God, then stakes are raised to a level where we come face to face with the spectre of sin'.[49] If we do overstep the limit, then, according to Shields, 'we will explicate this irrepressible tendency in terms of "sin" '.[50] In effect, by stepping over the limit we are not simply making a philosophical error, but we are also stepping over God's will into a serious transgression of questioning and denying the 'sovereignty' of God. Shields says, 'metaphysics ... is a work that does not respect the underlying powers which sustain people's lives. It turns us away from our roots [and] represents our profound refusal to acknowledge our limits and sources of meaning.'[51] So what Wittgenstein would call metaphysics in the *Tractatus* (where language does not connect to the simple object), Shields would call sin (where language does not connect with the pre-established conditions).

In the *Tractatus*, confusion results from language not connecting to elements of reality (simple objects), while in Shields's work confusion results from language not connecting with God's pre-established conditions. Consequently, as we struggle on the frontline of the battle for clarity in philosophy, we continually run up against the will of God and logical form, and if we cross this line we 'sin'. Shields draws his understanding of sin from Augustine, whereby Wittgenstein 'reflects a commitment to a basic Augustinian theodicy, where evil must have to do with our will since there can be no other source for evil in a world created by an all-powerful, supremely good Deity'.[52] Since Shields links philosophical confusion with sin, and sin with our will, the perplexing conclusion is that we choose philosophical confusion.

Shields wants to show that logical form is associated with God, and that philosophical confusion is associated with sin. He notes that 'our fallen state is nowhere more clearly evident than in the perpetual nature of our philosophical confusions'.[53] In order to understand the problem of linking philosophical confusion with sin, we need to be clear on how Shields relates the two. He remarks:

> The distinctive status of philosophical problems for Wittgenstein is similar to the status of evil and sin for Augustine – although they have no place in the ultimate, God-given scheme of things, they take on tremendous importance because they represent the perversity of the human will.[54]

Philosophical problems, which are a result of philosophical confusions, are not, for Shields, simply a lack of philosophical acumen; rather, they are a sin which represents the depravity of the human will. Sin, according to Shields, and along Augustinian lines, has no substance, and therefore resides solely in the perversion of the will.[55] Consider the case of stealing. We know, generally speaking, that it is wrong to steal. Nevertheless, we may wilfully decide to steal someone's belonging while knowing that it is a sin to do so. This is what giving in to temptation is: to give in to that which we know we should not do. If we are under the illusion that it is acceptable to steal from another, if we do not accept the rules in the first place, then it is not falling into temptation. Shields therefore writes, 'sin does not generally include things like miscalculations, misunderstandings and other errors due to human stupidity'.[56] It is a requirement to know it is wrong to steal in order to fall into the temptation to steal.

This understanding of sin is certainly acceptable (in a narrow sense), but in order to understand the deeper problem with Shields's conception of sin as placed upon philosophical confusion, the distinction between a mistake and a deliberate choice must be clarified. A mistake implies that we know the correct rules and, in contrast to sinning, try to follow these rules, yet unwittingly err. Rhees notes:

> Where he [Wittgenstein] spoke of a 'misunderstanding of the logic of language', obviously he did not mean that when I fall into this misunderstanding I show that I do not know the language. It is only because I understand the grammar of words like 'cause' and 'thinking' – only then is it possible (logically possible) to misunderstand them.[57]

To illustrate, in the case of a grammatical mistake, we can be corrected because we actually follow – or at least try to follow – the rules of grammar, we do not wilfully disobey the rules. Shields would agree with Rhees in that a mistake does require us to know the rules, just as in the case of falling into the temptation to steal requires us to know the law. However, in the case of stealing, although we know the law, we wilfully disobey it. Augustine says, for example, that he stole pears from a tree, not because he was hungry, but even worse: 'our real pleasure consisted in doing something that was forbidden'.[58] When Augustine stole the pears, it was not a mistake; he knew the law, but perversely chose to not follow it.

Shields ties his conception of sin – which is not like a grammatical mistake – to philosophical confusion, where our perverse will chooses the philosophical confusion, just as Augustine chose to steal the pears. He points out the significance of deciding to follow the temptation and places the responsibility directly upon the individual. If the act was an illusion or mistake, then responsibility decreases: 'Part of the inadequacy of speaking of philosophical problems solely in terms of illusions is that it obscures the responsibility of the deceived persons ...'[59] Furthermore, Shields says, 'in the Judeo-Christian tradition, illusions are usually perpetuated by external forces without an active compliance of the deceived, who are then usually considered morally blameless victims'.[60] In contrast to being 'morally blameless', Shields wants to adhere strongly to the idea of deliberate submission, where falling into temptation means we willingly pursue the transgression with complete lucidity. Shields writes: 'It must not simply be a matter of our failure to solve a riddle or dispel an illusion. Our transgressions can only be the result of a kind of perversity, where something is said, done, or desired in open defiance of the will of God.'[61] Elsewhere, Shields says, 'this blindness is not caused by mere ignorance, but by a perverse will that knows the good but prefers lower things'.[62] Within Shields's theory there is no excuse for transgressions, but there is an explanation, namely, our perverse will. It is clear that he understands sin and philosophical confusions as a deliberate decision of a rebellious will[63] which knows what is required, but directs itself towards other things.[64] Shields clearly states that he is not discussing a mistake, and this can make sense when applied to a common understanding of sin (e.g. stealing), but ends in puzzlement when applied to philosophy.

The idea of deep illusions and confusions are foreign to Shields who writes, 'Wittgenstein's treatment of philosophical problems in terms of "illusions" ... is generally inadequate.'[65] For Shields, illusions cannot adequately explain philosophical problems, only a perverse will can:

Although Wittgenstein does occasionally speak of philosophical problems as illusions, such ways of speaking are few compared to his tendency to speak of a perversive will. He constantly shows he is aware of a tension between the right understanding and what we *want* to see.[66]

According to Shields we know what is correct, but we want and choose the erroneous by means of our perverse will. Yet Wittgenstein recognizes the difficulty of seeing clearly: 'How hard it is to see what is *right in front of my eyes*!'[67] Furthermore, Wittgenstein says 'a philosophical problem has the form "I don't know my way about",'[68] not 'I know my way about, but choose to not follow it.' Rather than clearly seeing the correct 'path' we are often like Wittgenstein's fly in the bottle, in which case we keep bumping against the limits and not seeing the correct 'path', rather than clearly seeing the way out but choosing to keep bumping against the sides of the bottle.[69]

Shields does not accept the idea that we cannot see clearly since that would imply that we have not given assent to all the prerequisite rules *before* we used language. He says 'meaning is given like a gift, or a covenant of God made toward the undeserving, and one must either accept it or reject the possibility of meaningful language'.[70] Shields's point is clear: we either 'accept' or 'reject' meaning, and this is not a passive rejection. Hence, the problem according to Shields, is not a mistake, but the wilful desire to go beyond the limit. He says, 'the real danger is not occasional mistakes or the existence of intermediate cases but the utter failure to accept rules, to submit to the requisite authority, in the first place'.[71] For Shields, we know what is correct, but nonetheless choose what is incorrect.

We find a similar understanding in Calvin's work: 'The knowledge of God has been naturally implanted in the human mind', and therefore 'makes the reprobate without excuse.'[72] Shields and Calvin place a God-given awareness as fundamental to meaning, then, if we do not follow the correct meaning we do so knowingly with our perverse will. In other words, we understand the ethical, but choose the sin: we know the dictates of logical grammar, but choose philosophical confusion.[73] It is right to note that we must know the correct grammar before we can reject it, but it seems very odd to imagine an individual knowingly rejecting meaningful language and choosing the incorrect grammar.[74] While we can image someone choosing the incorrect deed and stealing, it is almost inconceivable to imagine someone choosing the incorrect grammar and continually speaking or writing nonsense on purpose. It may be more accurate, following Shields's argument, to call someone who rejects meaningful language unsound, not a sinner.

Shields does not accept the depth of philosophical problems (illusions), and he does not accept the depth of sin (original sin). He thereby ends up with sin and philosophical confusions being a surface decision, in which case the fault lies in a perverse will, in contrast to a deep illusion in our thinking. A more profitable discussion of Wittgenstein would discuss the depth of philosophical illusions and original sin, in which case it is not so much a problem of a perverse will choosing the incorrect act or philosophical confusion, but a deep problem that needs to be corrected and where the will is often unaware of the depth of confusion and sin (like Wittgenstein's fly in the bottle). But then Shields would lose the impact of his interpretation of personal responsibility, and since he does not want to lose the impact of personal decision and accountability, he regards the idea of original sin as unreasonable. Shields sees original sin as a 'troubling image. The idea that the sins of the parents are visited upon their children has become foreign and repugnant to most of us – it goes against both our laws and our sense of justice.'[75] Instead of a deep understanding of sin, Shields understands original sin as 'not simply a matter of being mysteriously blamed now for something Adam and Eve did long ago, but rather a matter of recognizing our continuing complicity in their act of disobedience and alienation'.[76] Shields's conception of language requires God's will and logical form as preliminary; therefore, we must know what is right and wrong prior to our use of language. If we err we do so knowingly – there is no excuse.

Shields's conclusions regarding the association of God's will and logical form in his discussion of Wittgenstein's writing, as based on the *Tractatus*, are unconvincing. Shields's analysis argues an interpretive link between logical form (as the transcendental) and God's will, and consequently philosophical confusion and sin. Discussions of logical form and God may be arguable, but his resultant linking of philosophical confusion and sin is inconceivable, particularly since he is not simply offering a comparison or an analogy for Wittgenstein's writings, but considers himself to have discovered the quintessence of Wittgenstein's entire corpus, claiming it to be not only ethical but religious.[77] He moves the Tractarian analysis even further from logic – where Wittgenstein intended it to remain – to discourse regarding the relation between human beings and God in the context of sin.

Shields's understanding of logical form, through the lens of the say/show distinction, propounds the basics, but it falters on two levels: it dismisses the application of language (perhaps unwittingly), and it overtly incorporates religion. In his desire for the absolute, Shields refuses to accept the vagueness of propositions and consequently he mistakenly attributes a greater significance to *a priori* foundations than ordinary language. Shields is riveted to the idea of logical syntax as king and ruler of our wayward world. He writes:

> In Wittgenstein's writings on logic and grammar I will seek traces, not of the kind and gentle father, but of the Law-Giver, and the terrible, demanding, and humanly incomprehensible God of the Judaic prophets – the God who judges individuals, cities and nations and then destroys or preserves them as he chooses, accountable to no one.[78]

This is the God Shields seeks in Wittgenstein's writings, a distant and removed power that judges the philosophically confused and sustains the philosophically clear. Shields's religious picture forces its own meaning on his project; his conclusion of Wittgenstein's thought as religious is not a discovery, but a forced agenda. Wittgenstein recognizes the problem of seeking such ideals: 'The more narrowly we examine actual language, the sharper becomes the conflict between it and our requirement. (For the crystalline purity of logic was, of course, not a *result of our investigation*: it was a requirement.)'[79] Shields's understanding of religion is not being questioned here, nor is his interpretation of the *Tractatus*; rather, what is being questioned are the ideas that the two should be forced together, and that Wittgenstein's entire corpus of writings continue the Tractarian line of reasoning and clearly show, through logical analysis, the God of the Judaic prophets.

While Wittgenstein simply intended to clarify language through the Tractarian say/show distinction, Shields goes further and finds God's will in the status of the shown, and sin – like philosophical confusion – defined by the limit of what can be said. Indeed, he says, 'if philosophical problems infest the world like original sin, then when we do philosophy we are putting ourselves in that venerable tradition equivalent to the heroic tradition [of saints and prophets]'.[80] Shields wrongly attributes to the *Tractatus* a connection with God and sin that Wittgenstein does not hold, and he disregards the development of Wittgenstein's thought regarding the importance of the contexts of language applications.

Wittgenstein's post-*Tractatus* thought

Wittgenstein's later philosophy provides a more suitable context than his early philosophy for discussions of a 'religious point of view'. For example, his later philosophy will be shown, like a religious point of view, to not be a type of scientism (e.g. they are not *theories*, nor do they create theories). To profitably discuss and further develop the relation between Wittgenstein's later philosophy and a religious point of view – and in contrast to Shields's project – it is necessary to first acknowledge the distinct nature of Wittgenstein's later understanding of language, and his later conception of the role of philosophy.

Although the primary shift in Wittgenstein's understanding of language occurs after the *Tractatus*, we nevertheless find hints in the *Tractatus* itself that Wittgenstein begins to explore the relation between logic and its application. Wittgenstein remarks: 'a sign does not determine a logical form unless it is taken together with its logical-symbolical employment'.[81] If there is no use for a sign then there is no meaning.[82] The sign in the proposition must be understood as employed in order to see the connection between the proposition and the world. In other words, employment cannot be understood as logical form or syntax alone since the actual application is necessary for meaning: 'logic must have contact with its application'.[83] Logic does not operate alone; the use of a proposition is its application, and it is a picture which corresponds to a state of affairs.

Nevertheless, the Tractarian picture is based on a conception of truth and falsity in which a system of complete analysis can determine what is and is not a proposition, as if there is no need to pay attention to the actual use and purpose of the proposition. Wittgenstein comments on his former perception of logic:

> There seemed to pertain to logic a peculiar depth – a universal significance. Logic lay, it seemed, at the bottom of all the sciences. – For logical investigation explores the nature of all things. It seeks to see the bottom of all things and is not meant to concern itself whether what actually happens is this or that.[84]

In contrast to an explanation of atomic principles, the later Wittgenstein points out that it is a bad picture to say that a proposition is whatever can be true or false, as if what is true or false determines what is or is not a proposition.[85] Indeed, Wittgenstein became dissatisfied with the idea of any *theory* to explain language:

> Formerly, I myself spoke of a 'complete analysis', and I used to believe that philosophy had to give a definite dissection of propositions so as to set out clearly all their connections and remove all possibility of misunderstanding. I spoke as if there were a calculus in which such a dissection would be possible ... At the root of all this there was a false and idealized picture of the use of language.[86]

The world and language do not connect via the Tractarian view of independent elementary propositions, which are either true or false; rather, propositions are internally related, and they reflect the logic of language through use, not that which underlies language. It is no longer the truth functions of elementary propositions that reflect the logical undergirding of language towards the end of an explanation that are significant, it is the actual use of language towards description that becomes prominent. The conceptual framework of Logical Positivism, and in general an exclusively scientific world-view, fell into the background as the actual nature of language becomes prominent.

We may attribute a certain 'purity' to logic as somehow being independent from the world, but this conception does not accurately reflect the significance of logic at work in the world, for it is only in the world that logic can have any foothold. Thus, as Peter Winch rightly notes, that which can be said is

> limited by certain formal requirements centering around the demand for consistency. But these formal requirements tell us nothing about what in particular is to *count* as consistency, just as the rules of the predicate calculus limit but do not determine what are to be the proper values of p, q, etc. We can only determine this by investigating the wider context of the life in which the activities in question are carried on.[87]

The distinction between understanding language through external connections, in contrast to the language-games, can be illustrated as follows: take, for example, p . -p, which is a contradiction, but when related to the world may be 'true'. For instance, it is snowing and it is not snowing, a type of precipitation that is best defined as rain-snow (sleet). Logic may remain 'pure' in a textbook or in rationalizations, but when applied to the world, it is put to work and cannot remain as a strict binary in abstraction. Indeed, this is why Bertrand Russell, in conversation with Wittgenstein, often exclaimed: 'Logic is Hell!'[88]

When we look to see what is actually happening with our use of language, when we describe language rather than explain it, we must look at language comprehensively instead of reflecting upon the truth or falsity of a proposition. Take, for example, Wittgenstein's comment to Waismann:

I once wrote 'A proposition is like a ruler laid against reality.' Only the outermost graduating marks touch the object to be measured. I would now rather say: a *system* of propositions is laid against reality like a ruler. What I mean is this: when I lay a ruler against a spatial object, I lay all the graduating lines against it at the same time. It is not individual graduating lines that are laid beside it, but the whole scale.[89]

It was this turning to the internal relationships between propositions, in contrast to independent truth and falsity, that made Wittgenstein aware of the truth-values as interdependent and forming a whole, namely the use of language. Accordingly, we do not start with a single independent proposition and then build our system; rather, we start with a system of propositions[90] – 'Philosophy is not laid down in sentences, but in language.'[91]

The early Wittgenstein says that there is a certain unity in language as based on the underlying structure of simple objects, but in his later writings he regards this as mistaken: there is no '*preconceived idea* of crystalline purity'.[92] In the *Tractatus* that which underlies language is significant, with logical form as the absolute measure for unity, but Wittgenstein's later thought points to the significance of that which is found through the use of language, still logical form, but now unity is found through the use of language in the language-games. In other words, logical form changes; formerly it was the underpinning of language, which enables the name to link with the object, but later it became that which is known through the use of language. No longer does an atomistic structure built from a simple object to complex propositions seem plausible for Wittgenstein;[93] instead there is an entire system of language right before us, and that is our starting-point.

The change in Wittgenstein's thought conflicts with a foundational viewpoint. His understanding of logic and language changes from a strict Tractarian system to a more fluid notion of language as used in varying contexts. He notes:

> The grammar of a language isn't recorded and doesn't come into existence until language has already been spoken by human beings for a *long* time. Similarly, primitive games are played without their rules being codified, and even without a single rule being formulated.[94]

Compare this with, for example, Shields's comment: 'Wittgenstein describes a world in which the rules that prescribe the use of meaningful expressions are sharply defined in terms of a preexisting horizon.'[95] Not only is it difficult to conceive of a point in time at which we give assent to Shields's pre-established conditions, but the rules are not even established until we use language – in contrast to the necessity of prescriptive rules. In contrast to Shields's and Ackermann's conception of language being determined in advance and not dependent on our decisions or exploration of the world,[96] Wittgenstein makes it clear that language forms through human activity. This changes the view of philosophical confusion from Shields's idea of transgressing God's will (the pre-established conditions and prescriptive rules) to simply using language outside its particular context. Granted, there are rules for our use of language in a particular context, but that very use of language formed the rules, the rules did not pre-determine language.

Trying to determine which is first – logic and grammatical rules or language, or the knowledge of God or worship – is futile, as D. Z. Phillips observes:

> The argument appears circular and contradictory if one thinks of either logic or language as being prior to the other. But as in the case of the child's stories and the concept of God, to ask which came first is to ask a senseless question. As soon as one has language one has logic

which determines what can and what cannot be said in that language without being prior to it.[97]

To ask which is first, logic or language, is as pointless as trying to give logical priority to an assent to the pre-established conditions before using language. Instead, we only have the language we use. We can only understand logical grammar through our use of language, and we can only understand religion through worship. Do we first ascertain that God exists, and then worship God and practise a particular religion, or is God instead found in that very language of worship and practice? Likewise, how can we know the rules of grammar before using language? One way to implement foundational theories like Shields's, is to apply them to learning a second language, in which case we do know a logical grammar before saying anything in the second language. Or if we practise a particular religion and then compare another religion's conception of God with our own. But the implication of Shields's theory is that we must give assent to logical grammar before we use language: 'we need to accept these conditions [logical grammar] before we can do or say anything at all'.[98] This is entirely different from saying that we learn logical grammar (or about God) by 'doing' and 'saying' within the language.

What becomes important in Wittgenstein's later understanding of language is the form of life for language in contrast to a rule-governed logical form. Wittgenstein's comment regarding a machine can be aptly applied to foundational theories:

> We talk as if these parts could only move in this way, as if they could not do anything else. How is this – do we forget the possibility of their bending, breaking off, melting, and so on? Yes; in many cases we don't think of that at all.[99]

Although it is correct to note that the language-games in a sense determine (grammatical) forms, it is because of the 'everyday use' and 'ordinary meaning' (which can change) that this is so, not because of some underlying structure. Wittgenstein's point is that language is a matter of human convention.[100] He says,

> the rules of grammar are arbitrary in the same sense as the choice of

a unit of measurement. But that means no more than that the choice is independent of the length of the objects to be measured and that the choice of one unit is not 'true' and another 'false' in the way that a statement of length is true or false.[101]

The choice to use a particular unit of measurement is a matter of human convention, not foundational strictures (i.e. God's will, or the simple object).

Logic and meaning are beyond our personal control, but they are not beyond humanity; rather, we develop language as we go along.[102] Exactness is what we have when we understand each other in ordinary conversation; for instance, when in our everyday conversation we ask for five apples and the shopkeeper simply gives us five apples.[103] How do we accept or reject meaning when it is what arises from our social life; for example, how can we accept the use of the word 'five'? Perhaps we could reject the use of the word 'five', but that could only happen after it has been used correctly. And if we use the word 'five' correctly, then at what point did we accept the correct use? Exactness is not something that stands outside our conversations which we then use to judge how exact our conversation is – as if we can look at the picture on a package of seeds and think that that is exactly how our tree will look without giving any credence to other possibilities, such as the strong west wind that blows all the branches to the east. The significance is the form of life, not God's will as a rule governor.

Language is not subsequent to accepting the logical grammar;[104] rather, Wittgenstein sees logical grammar in the language we use: 'It is what humans beings *say* that is true and false; and they agree in the *language* they use. That is not agreement in opinions but in form of life.'[105] If there is any notion of transgression, then what we transgress are not God's pre-established grammatical rules (by denying the connection between the God-given pre-established conditions and language), as if we had in fact mastered the essence of language conceptually, but the use of language in our social life. We can speak of established conditions *of* language (i.e. our use of language establishes the conditions for what is and is not correct linguistic use), but it is entirely different to say that there are pre-established conditions *for* language. The former does not place any logical priorities for rules or language use, while the latter defines additional elements that are prior to language use, and to which language must be fixed (e.g. simple object and pre-established conditions).[106]

What lies at the bottom of language, as it were, is not the simple object, God's will, pre-established conditions, or prescriptive rules, but our acting in life. Wittgenstein writes:

> What *counts* as a test? – 'But is this an adequate test? And, if so, must it not be recognizable as such in logic?' – As if giving grounds did not come to an end sometime. But the end is not an ungrounded presupposition: it is an ungrounded way of acting.[107]

Furthermore,

> Giving grounds, however justifying the evidence, comes to an end; – but the end is not certain propositions striking us immediately as true, i.e. it is not a kind of *seeing* on our part; it is our *acting* which lies at the bottom of the language-game.[108]

Therefore, when there is a confusion in language, it is a confusion within a particular use of language in life rather than a violation against 'language itself' (as if there is one absolute language), the pre-established conditions, or God's will. The language we use is not determined by an *a priori* structure, but by our acting, and it follows that language can have various forms.[109] Consequently, there can be multiple confusions by using words outside their contexts, like using a tool made for a different fitting or size, or by not taking into account that a certain word has become, so to speak, broken or bent. We understand language through using language; likewise language develops through that very use. Wittgenstein notes this change in his thought:

> It is interesting to compare the multiplicity of the tools in language and of the ways they are used, the multiplicity of kinds of word and sentence, with what logicians have said about the structure of language. (Including the author of the *Tractatus Logico-Philosophicus*).[110]

These actions and tools bring to light the idea of the language-game where, according to Wittgenstein, 'the term "language-*game*" is meant to bring into prominence the fact that the *speaking* of a language is part of an activity or a form of life'.[111] Indeed, we can only think of language if we can think of a form of life.[112]

Once again, imagine, for example, a tree. Its roots are indeed 'below' the surface, but no tree can remain unaffected by the environment (e.g. wind, sun, rain, temperature). We can take two identical spruce seeds, plant them in different environments – for instance in the wind-swept west coast, or in a sheltered inland habitat – and the result will be two trees that do not grow the same. It is important to note that even if we say there is a prescriptive rule in the genetic code of the seed that will form the trees (the two identical seeds), the trees may nonetheless change through time by their interaction in the environment, just as language can change through developing uses of language. We interact with the trees, not simply with some ideal understanding of the seed. Indeed, the seed has taken on life in the world (bending and breaking) and cannot even be pointed to. The use of the tree resides in the tree itself, not the seed. Hence:

> There are *countless* kinds: countless different kinds of use of what we call 'symbols', 'words', 'sentences'. And this multiplicity is not something fixed, given once for all; but new types of language, new language-games, as we may say, come into existence, and others become obsolete and get forgotten.[113]

Elsewhere, Wittgenstein notes: 'What I am opposed to is the concept of some ideal exactitude given us *a priori*, as it were. At different times we have different ideals of exactitude; none of them is supreme.'[114]

Wittgenstein's point is that there is no general theory, that the variety in life of different applications for language does not allow any strict system to determine language outside of life. He sees that he has not given the essence of the language-game which is common to all language-games either.[115] Instead they are like the many strands of a rope with no one strand being the essence of the rope.[116] The language-games are diverse and related to each other in many different ways:

> Our language can be seen as an ancient city: a maze of little streets and squares, of old and new houses, and of houses with additions from

various periods; and this surrounded by a multitude of new boroughs with straight regular streets and uniform houses.[117]

Language is a labyrinth of paths.[118]

Language emerges through the multiple paths of life, not from logical syntax. In light of Wittgenstein's continual insistence on the heterogeneity of language and its dependence on our use, it is difficult to accept Shields's Tractarian reading of pre-established conditions and formal unity. Indeed, if we do not accept Shields's Tractarian logic as applied to the entire corpus of Wittgenstein's work, then the foundation of Shields's project is brought into question. To posit foundational strictures clearly underestimates the value of understanding developed through our use of language, as Winch sees: 'The criteria of logic are not a direct gift of God, but arise out of, and are only intelligible in the context of, ways of living and modes of social life.'[119]

Language is obviously not known *a priori*; it is only through our practice of language in the world that we can grasp any sense of language, and make any subsequent judgements as to whether we are using language correctly or not. Rather than language being understood through connections with additional elements (the simple object or pre-established conditions) and transgressed by not attaching to these elements, language is brought down to our worldly affairs where it is used, created and misused within language-games. The relation between a state of affairs and our propositions is found in the language-games, not in an external structure.

An understanding of Wittgenstein's later view of philosophy helps bring to light its 'therapeutic' nature. Indeed, Wittgenstein says the 'philosopher's treatment of a question is like the treatment of an illness'.[120] In order to prescribe a treatment it is necessary, of course, to first understand the illness. For example, Wittgenstein's later conception of language shifts the problem of confusion from stepping over the limit of a Tractarian formal unity, to the problem of using language outside the language-game. When language is abstracted from the language-games it is out of work and confusion is the result: 'the confusions which occupy us arise when language is like an engine idling, not when it is doing work'.[121]

Wittgenstein's emphasis on language-game activities may appear to result in a less rigorous conception of philosophy than one that tends to the details of an underlying logical syntax. However, the philosophical confusion that results from language not functioning within a language-game, and instead being abstracted to a metaphysical realm, is a serious concern for Wittgenstein. He writes: 'the problems arising through a misinterpretation of our forms of language have the character of *depth*. They are deep disquietudes; their roots are as deep in us as the forms of our language and their significance is as great as the importance of our language.'[122] The depth of philosophical confusion is tied to the fact that it is not like a scientific problem. That is, it will not be answered by a hypothetical discovery (as is the case for a scientific problem), nor can it be treated by further analysis into an underlying logical syntax or transcendental realm.

To understand the nature of philosophical confusion, and how it is to be treated in Wittgenstein's later thought, it is helpful to once again note his observation, 'a philosophical problem has the form: "I don't know my way about." '[123] It is clear that someone who is not familiar with the landscape is not helped by constructing theories, but by becoming familiar with their concrete surroundings. Similarly, metaphysical theories and explanations do not resolve philosophical confusion since the 'essence' of language is not something 'beneath the surface', but is 'open to view'.[124] Thus, the best treatment is to become familiar with one's surroundings; that is, the language-game. In Wittgenstein's later conception of philosophy confusion is not resolved by an analysis of logical syntax or by a transcendental realm, but by paying attention to the use of language in the form of life. Wittgenstein writes:

> when philosophers use a word – 'knowledge', 'being' ... and try to grasp the essence of the thing, one must always ask oneself: is the word ever actually used in this way in the language-game which is its original home? – What *we* do is to bring words back from their metaphysical to their everyday use.[125]

Once again, if we are unfamiliar with the terrain, the treatment is not to theorize, but to become familiar with the rough ground. Hence, 'philosophy simply puts everything before us, and neither explains nor deduces anything'.[126] The treatment for the illness of philosophical confusion is not a matter of ratiocination, but of description.

This may seem to be an insignificant aim for philosophy – that it simply describes the use of language – but the treatment is as serious as the illness. The 'therapeutic' nature of Wittgenstein's later philosophy is certainly not a type of quietism. Wittgenstein says, 'what we find out in philosophy is trivial; it does not teach us new facts, only science does that. But the proper synopsis of these trivialities is enormously difficult, and has immense importance. Philosophy is in fact the synopsis of the trivialities.'[127] His later conception of philosophy may seem to be modest (in that it deals with trivialities and is not scientific), but its 'therapeutic' nature is far from subtle. Wittgenstein writes:

> where does our investigation get its importance from, since it seems to only destroy everything interesting, that is, all that is great and important? (As it were all the buildings, leaving behind only bits of stone and rubble.) What we are destroying is nothing but houses of cards and we are clearing up the ground of language on which they stand.[128]

Wittgenstein's later philosophy actively destroys 'houses of cards', that is, superficial theories and explanations. It is important to note, however, that the 'therapeutic' aspect of Wittgenstein's later philosophy does not entail creating new buildings to replace those that have been destroyed. He says, 'all that philosophy can do is destroy idols'; and importantly, 'that means not creating a new one'.[129] A treatment must not be another disease in disguise – the treatment is not to construct further idols in an attempt to resolve the problem of idols. A therapy must not advance further philosophical idols such as an underlying foundation for language (e.g. simple object) or follow the idolization of the scientific method as the only proper technique for philosophy (e.g. logical positivism).

Wittgenstein's understanding of language and his conception of the role of philosophy change in his later thought. For example, in the *Tractatus* Wittgenstein notes that the method of the philosopher is to 'give meaning to certain signs in his propositions'.[130] The meaning of a proposition is displayed once it is analysed into elementary propositions with specific signs. However, in his later thought he says: 'What is your aim in philosophy? – To show the fly the way out of the fly-bottle.'[131] The fly-bottle can represent the philosophical confusion of misleading theories and explanations, such as the scientific method of Logical Positivism. The way out of the fly-bottle is not discovered with 'new information, but by arranging what we have always known'.[132] Philosophical confusion is not corrected by mending one theory with another theory; rather, the confusion requires a therapy to eradicate it. Wittgenstein says, 'there is not *a* philosophical method, though there are indeed methods, like different therapies'.[133] His later philosophy is 'therapeutic' for philosophical confusion, not by offering a patch for an unsatisfactory theory, but by discerning the illness, applying a therapy, and then working backwards to the opening of the fly-bottle.

Towards a post-Tractarian discussion of Wittgenstein's 'religious point of view'

There is a unity in language, that is, language is not simply an arbitrary will-o'-the-wisp phenomenon, but the unity is not a formal unity grounded by pre-established conditions as Shields thinks. Wittgenstein's later philosophy places our form of life as the mode of unity; that is, language is not an isolated phenomenon, but is interrelated. Or from another angle, we can discuss unity via our form of life which reflects the unity, and we can do so without transcendent terminology; there is no need to bring in the pre-established conditions to secure unity, or to explain unity. Nevertheless, Shields sees Wittgenstein's philosophy in a transcendent and 'religious' light, and inverts Wittgenstein's remark – theology as grammar[134] – by claiming that we should understand 'grammar as theology, as the study of the will of God'.[135]

Shields's project makes it clear that an alternate study of Wittgenstein's philosophy and a 'religious point of view' is required. Wittgenstein's thought must not be confounded with religion or reduced to a Tractarian framework. Since Shields's conception of Wittgenstein's philosophy is misguided, he also chooses an unsuitable religious viewpoint (i.e. Calvinism and the Reformed tradition). In contrast to Shields's project, Wittgenstein's later understanding of language and conception of philosophy must be clearly addressed to facilitate the investigation into a suitable religious analogy.

What connects Wittgenstein's later philosophy with a 'religious point of view', and as will be shown Hebraic thought in particular, is their similar divergence from an exclusively scientific world-view, theorizing and excessive explanations. For example, Wittgenstein says, 'it was true to say that our considerations could not be scientific ones ... we may not advance any kind of theory. There must not be anything hypothetical in our considerations. We must do away with all explanation, and description alone must take its place.'[136] Similarly (within a particular strand of Hebraic thought that will be developed in the fourth chapter), Gerald Bruns notes:

> In Midrash authority is social rather than methodological and thus is holistic rather than atomic or subject-centered: the whole dialogue, that is the institution of midrash itself – rabbinic practice – is authoritative, and what counts is conformity with this practice rather than correspondence to some external rule or theory concerning the content of interpretation as such.[137]

Even the written Torah is not clearly more authoritative than social authority and practice: 'the rabbinic enactments are Torah, and in a certain respect are "more weighty" than the laws of the written Torah'.[138] In Wittgenstein's and Hebraic thought the form of life and concrete practices will be shown to take precedence over conceptions of a formal unity and transcendental realms. Neither Wittgenstein's later philosophy nor a religious perspective, such as Hebraic thought, is a *theory* or a method for constructing theories.

Wittgenstein's later understanding of language and conception of the role of philosophy require a religious point of view to be discussed in terms that are dramatically different from those offered by Shields. What is required is a post-*Tractatus* discussion of Wittgenstein's philosophy as *analogous* to a religious point of view. The following chapters will build on Wittgenstein's later conception of language and philosophy, and will ultimately show that they can be fruitfully compared analogically with a religious point of view in terms of a particular strand of Hebraic thought.

Endnotes

1   Wittgenstein, *Philosophical Investigations*, viii.
2   Shields, *Logic and Sin*, 91.
3   *Ibid.*, 7.
4   *Ibid.*, 5.
5   Rhees, *Discussions of Wittgenstein*, 9.
6   No attempt is made in this discussion to make an original contri-
    bution to the extensive scholarship on the *Tractatus*; rather, the
    intention is simply to state the rudimentary principles of Tractarian
    logic in order to understand Shields's theory and as a background
    to Wittgenstein's later philosophy.
7   Wittgenstein, *Tractatus Logico-Philosophicus*, 4.016.
8   *Ibid.*, 4.01.
9   *Ibid.*, 2.223.
10 *Ibid.*, 5, 5.01.
11 *Ibid.*, 5.3.
12 *Ibid.*, 3.203.
13 *Ibid.*, 3.22.
14 *Ibid.*, 3.144.
15 *Ibid.*, 2.1511.
16 Ludwig Wittgenstein, *Notebooks*, ed. G. H. von Wright and G. E. M.
    Anscombe, trans. G. E. M. Anscombe (Oxford: Blackwell, 1979),
    62.
17 Wittgenstein, *Tractatus Logico-Philosophicus*, 2.0211.
18 *Ibid.*, 1.1–1.12.
19 *Ibid.*, 4.26.
20 *Ibid.*, 4.001.
21 *Ibid.*, 7.
22 Paul Engelmann, *Letters From Ludwig Wittgenstein, with a Memoir*, ed.
    B. F. McGuinness, trans. L. Furtmüller (Oxford: Basil Blackwell,
    1967), 143–4.
23 Wittgenstein, *Tractatus Logico-Philosophicus*, 4.12.
24 *Ibid.*
25 *Ibid.*, 2.18.
26 *Ibid.*, 4.1212.
27 *Ibid.*, 2.172.

28   *Ibid.*, 4.121.

29   *Ibid.*, 5.43.

30   *Ibid.*, 6.522.

31   *Ibid.*, 6.41.

32   Engelmann, *Letters From Wittgenstein*, 97.

33   Wittgenstein, *Tractatus Logico-Philosophicus*, 6.42.

34   Shields, *Logic and Sin*, ix.

35   *Ibid.*, x, 2.

36   *Ibid.*, 6.

37   *Ibid.*, x.

38   *Ibid.*, 8–9.

39   *Ibid.*, 114.

40   *Ibid.*, 33.

41   *Ibid.*, 66.

42   *Ibid.*, 68.

43   *Ibid.*, 66.

44   *Ibid.*, 45.

45   *The Philosophical Writings of Descartes*, trans. J. Cottingham, R. Stoothoff and D. Murdoch (Cambridge: Cambridge University Press, 1985), 2:49.

46   Wittgenstein, *Tractatus Logico-Philosophicus*, 2.0201–2.021. This view changes, as we will see in Wittgenstein's later writings, where the meaning of a name does not depend on the existence of the object or a substitute.

47   Wittgenstein, *Notebooks*, 62.

48   Shields, *Logic and Sin*, 90.

49   *Ibid.*, 56.

50   *Ibid.*, 29.

51   *Ibid.*, 68.

52   *Ibid.*, 35.

53   *Ibid.*, 106.

54   *Ibid.*, 64.

55   *Ibid.*

56   *Ibid.*, 57.

57   Rush Rhees, *Rush Rhees on Religion and Philosophy*, ed. D. Z. Phillips and Mario von der Ruhr (Cambridge: Cambridge University Press, 1997), 85.

58 Saint Augustine, *Confessions*, trans. by R. S. Pine-Coffin (London: Penguin Books, 1961), bk 2, ch. 4.

59 Shields, *Logic and Sin*, 56.

60 *Ibid.*

61 *Ibid.*, 57.

62 *Ibid.*, 64.

63 *Ibid.*

64 *Ibid.*, 66.

65 *Ibid.*, 52.

66 *Ibid.*, 55.

67 Wittgenstein, *Culture and Value*, 39e.

68 Wittgenstein, *Philosophical Investigations*, § 123.

69 *Ibid.*, § 308.

70 Shields, *Logic and Sin*, 46.

71 *Ibid.*, 66.

72 Calvin, *John Calvin: Institutes of the Christian Religion*, trans. Henry Beveridge (London: Arnold Hatfield, 1599), bk 1, ch. 3, sec. 1.

73 Shields, *Logic and Sin*, 64.

74 The implications of Shields's Tractarian notion of knowing logical form and God's will *a priori* will be dealt with in detail in the following section, where Wittgenstein's later thought adds an argumentative application.

75 Shields, *Logic and Sin*, 62.

76 *Ibid.*

77 *Ibid.*, x.

78 *Ibid.*, 31.

79 Wittgenstein, *Philosophical Investigations*, § 107.

80 Shields, *Logic and Sin*, 63.

81 Wittgenstein, *Tractatus Logico-Philosophicus*, 3.327.

82 *Ibid.*, 3.328.

83 *Ibid.*, 5.557.

84 Wittgenstein, *Philosophical Investigations*, § 89.

85 *Ibid.*, § 136.

86 Ludwig Wittgenstein, *Philosophical Grammar*, ed. Rush Rhees, trans. Anthony Kenny (Oxford: Basil Blackwell, 1974), 211.

87 Peter Winch, *Ethics and Action* (London: Routledge & Kegan Paul, 1972), 35.

88   Wittgenstein, *Culture and Value*, 30e.

89   Ludwig Wittgenstein, in *Wittgenstein and the Vienna Circle*, Conversations recorded by Friedrich Waismann, ed. Brian McGuinness, trans. Joachim Schulte and Brian McGuinness (Oxford: Basil Blackwell, 1979), 63–4.

90   Ludwig Wittgenstein, *On Certainty*, ed. G. E. M. Anscombe and G. H. von Wright, trans. Denis Paul and G. E. M. Anscombe (Oxford: Basil Blackwell, 1979), 105.

91   Ludwig Wittgenstein, 'Sections 86–93 (pp. 405–35) of the so-called "Big Typescript"', ed. Heikki Nyman, trans. C. G. Luckhardt and M. A. E. Aue, *Synthese*, 87, 1 (April, 1991), 6.

92   Wittgenstein, *Philosophical Investigations*, § 108.

93   Wittgenstein says, in the *Philosophical Investigations*, 'It makes no sense at all to speak absolutely of the "simple parts of a chair"' (§ 47). In other words, he is critiquing the idea of simplicity in the *Tractatus*, where the simple object is regarded as a necessary element for meaning, while his later thought saw meaning to reside in the complex ordinary language without any necessary recourse to the simple object. Just as we do not talk of an ear, tail, whisker, paw, etc., but of a cat, meaning is found in ordinary language, not the simple elements.

94   Wittgenstein, *Philosophical Grammar*, 62–3.

95   Shields, *Logic and Sin*, 56.

96   R. J. Ackermann, *Wittgenstein's City* (Amherst, MA: University of Massachusetts Press, 1988), 18–19.

97   D. Z. Phillips, *Wittgenstein and Religion* (London: Macmillan, 1993), 4.

98   Shields, *Logic and Sin*, 102.

99   Wittgenstein, *Philosophical Investigations*, § 193.

100 Wittgenstein, *Philosophical Grammar*, 190. See also Wittgenstein, *Philosophical Investigations*, § 355.

101 Wittgenstein, *Philosophical Grammar*, 185.

102 The problem of a private language will be discussed in Chapter 3.

103 Wittgenstein, *Philosophical Investigations*, § 1.

104 Shields, *Logic and Sin*, 90.

105 Wittgenstein, *Philosophical Investigations*, § 241.

106 We could say the established rules of grammar are pre-established

in the sense of being 'set up' before my initiation into a particular language-game, and before my existence; but if we follow this argument to its logical conclusion we still end up with the rules of language existing before the language-game, and before the existence of humans. In other words, we have prescriptive rules for language prior to language use.

107 Wittgenstein, *On Certainty*, 110.

108 *Ibid.*, 204.

109 Colin Lyas makes an interesting comment on this point: 'To use a language is necessarily to be creative in projecting what we have learned into ever new contexts. This is something *we* have to *do* and is not something, as some structuralists believed, that language does to us.' Colin Lyas, *Peter Winch* (Teddington: Acumen, 1999), 33.

110 Wittgenstein, *Philosophical Investigations*, § 23.

111 *Ibid.*

112 *Ibid.*

113 *Ibid.*

114 Wittgenstein, *Culture and Value*, 37e.

115 Wittgenstein, *Philosophical Investigations*, § 65.

116 *Ibid.*, § 67

117 *Ibid.*, § 18.

118 *Ibid.*, § 203.

119 Peter Winch, *The Idea of a Social Science* (London: Routledge & Kegan Paul, 1958), 100–1.

120 Wittgenstein, *Philosophical Investigations*, § 255. In Chapter 2 Malcolm will be shown to see an interesting analogy between illness within a philosophical context and a religious context.

121 Wittgenstein, *Philosophical Investigations*, § 132.

122 *Ibid.*, § 111.

123 *Ibid.*, § 123.

124 *Ibid.*, § 92.

125 *Ibid.*, § 116.

126 Wittgenstein, *Philosophical Investigations*, § 126.

127 Wittgenstein, *Wittgenstein's Lectures: 1930–1932*, from the notes of John King and Desmond Lee, ed. Desmond Lee (Chicago: University of Chicago Press, 1989), 26.

128 Wittgenstein, *Philosophical Investigations*, § 118.

129 Wittgenstein, 'Sections 86–93 (pp. 405–35) of the so-called "Big Typescript"', 9.

130 Wittgenstein, *Tractatus Logico-Philosophicus*, 6.53.

131 Wittgenstein, *Philosophical Investigations*, § 309.

132 *Ibid.*, § 109.

133 *Ibid.*, § 133.

134 *Ibid.*, § 373.

135 Shields, *Logic and Sin*, 50.

136 Wittgenstein, *Philosophical Investigations*, § 109. Wittgenstein says his thinking is different than that of the scientists, *Culture and Value*, 7e.

137 Gerald Bruns, *Hermeneutics Ancient and Modern* (New Haven: Yale University Press, 1992), 113. The strand of Hebraic thought selected for this discussion will be discussed further in Chapter 4.

138 Max Kadushin, *The Rabbinic Mind* (New York: Bloch, 1972), 356.

2

Wittgenstein's Later Philosophy and Religion

Wittgenstein's philosophy is sometimes thought to be religious, as evidenced by Shields, or at least to be analogous to religion. One major work that takes the latter option is Norman Malcolm's *Wittgenstein: A Religious Point of View?*, which focuses on Wittgenstein's remark to Drury: 'I am not a religious man but I cannot help seeing every problem from a religious point of view.'[1] What relation, if any, does this remark of Wittgenstein's have to his philosophy? Malcolm certainly thinks there is some relation between Wittgenstein's philosophy and a religious point of view: 'There is not strictly a religious point of view, but something analogous to a religious point of view, in Wittgenstein's later philosophical work.'[2] This is an obvious contrast to Shields, for whom Wittgenstein's philosophy *is* a religious point of view. Malcolm, not wanting to draw such a strong conclusion as Shields, remarks:

> Wittgenstein did much religious thinking: but religious thoughts do not figure in his detailed treatments of the philosophical problems. It would seem, therefore, that when he spoke of seeing those problems 'from a religious point of view', he did not mean that he conceived of them as religious problems, but instead that there was a similarity, or similarities, between his conception of philosophy and something that is characteristic of religious thinking.[3]

What we are discussing, then, in reference to Malcolm's work, is not that Wittgenstein's philosophy is the *same* as a religious point of view, as Shields thinks, but that there is a similarity between Wittgenstein's philosophy and a religious point of view. Shields's conception of Wittgenstein as a religious philosopher is questionable, obvious counter-examples being religious philosophers such as Augustine, Aquinas, and Maimonides, etc., all of whom imbued philosophy with religion and religion with philosophy. When compared with these authors Wittgenstein is seen for what he is, namely, a philosopher interested in the clarity of philosophy, not religious scholasticism. Wittgenstein has no goal to either support or reject religion; his only interest is to keep discussions, whether religious or not, clear.

If Shields's attempt to prove that Wittgenstein's philosophy *is* religious falters, then can we at least say there is a similarity between Wittgenstein's philosophy and religious thinking? Malcolm considers Wittgenstein's philosophy to have, on the basis of an analogy, a similar method to 'religious thinking'. Not that there is an equivalence, but there is at least some form of analogy that spurs Malcolm on to discuss what this similarity might be. Malcolm ties his project to his interpretation of Wittgenstein's later thought and in particular to the understanding that there is an end to explanation. This is the second contrast with Shields's work. Not only does Malcolm deny a direct equivalence between Wittgenstein's philosophy and a religious point of view, he also discusses this issue in terms of Wittgenstein's later thought. For example, Malcolm finds a similarity between the end of explanation, where, for instance, we cannot analyse a proposition down to a simple object and name, and the end of explanation as characterized by the religious believer's remark, 'It's God's will.'

Malcolm discusses the concept of the end of explanation in the context of the *Investigations* in particular, in contrast to Shields's focus on the *Tractatus*. Indeed, Malcolm contrasts the *Tractatus* and the *Investigations*, the former being strictly logical toward the end of defining language, and the latter recognizing and defining a limit to explanation. This later development of Wittgenstein's thought shifts the role of explanations from systematizing language to describing language, and it is this later idea of simply describing language and religion, in contrast to excessive explanation, that Malcolm holds: 'I will argue that there is an analogy between this conception of God [that God requires no explanation], and Wittgenstein's view of the human "language-games" and "forms of life" '.[4] In short, while the *Tractatus* discusses a method of logical analysis, the *Investigations* simply describe the language-games; just as in religion, for Malcolm, the believer does not have an explanation for God's actions.

The Tractarian perspective of the picture theory, as previously discussed, follows a logical path to explanation: non-elementary propositions being reduced to elementary propositions, to a name, and finally to a simple object. With the assurance of the simple object, the Tractarian logic assumes that it is possible to deductively conclude through logical analysis whether a proposition is an elementary proposition or a truth function of an elementary proposition. Then, if a proposition is true, it will be identical in structure to the thought it expresses. Through this deductive process, it is thought possible to understand the meaning of a proposition; there is an explanation for each proposition if we follow this rigorous path.

In contrast to this process of deduction, Malcolm considers language to be more fluid and contextual. There is no one basis, language, or explanation, as found in the Tractarian logic as 'a perfect order between language and reality'; accordingly, it was 'struck a crushing blow by the *Investigations*'.[5] No longer is it considered sufficient to trust the logical deduction that is offered in the *Tractatus*; instead, we must look at the surroundings and the context of the language used. Then we find meaning in the use of language, not by analysing language into names and simple objects. This is the later Wittgenstein's and Malcolm's point: we must get out from under the idea of explaining language and move towards the idea of describing language as we see in its use.

Malcolm's project rests on the proposal that there is an analogy between the limit of explanation as found in Wittgenstein's later philosophical thought, and a religious point of view.[6] Just as the *Investigations* highlight the limit of explanation, in contrast to the *Tractatus* which works through to the name and the simple object, so a religious point of view highlights the limit of explanation when, for instance, talking of God's actions. We can describe God's actions, but it is difficult, if not impossible, to justify or claim any foundational basis for them. Once again, we are left with describing what God has done, without recourse to some 'super' knowledge or logical argumentation that explains every action.

Wittgenstein's later philosophy as analogous to a 'religious point of view'

Malcolm's discussion of Wittgenstein's 'religious point of view' centres on

> Wittgenstein's conception of the grammar of language, and his view of what is paramount in religious life. First, in both there is an end to

explanation; second, in both there is an inclination to be amazed at the existence of something: third, into both there enters the notion of an 'illness'; fourth, in both, *doing, acting*, takes priority over intellectual understanding and reasoning.[7]

Malcolm focuses on Wittgenstein's later understanding of language which, as discussed previously, cannot be understood in terms of an exclusively scientific or explanatory system. Once again, Wittgenstein says, 'our considerations could not be scientific ones ... and we may not advance any kind of theory. There must not be anything hypothetical in our considerations. We must do away with all explanation, and description alone must take its place.'[8] This aspect of Wittgenstein's later thought, that there is an end to explanation, is found analogically within a religious context. For instance, a religious person may say 'It is in the hands of God' in response to adversity; not as an explanation, as if it then made sense that something bad has happened, but instead as a statement that, in effect, God is with them through the good and bad. Neither Wittgenstein's later philosophy nor the statement 'It is in the hands of God' attempt to explain or deduce anything; rather, they simply describe how things are.[9] The limit of explanation within a philosophical and religious context is the cornerstone of Malcolm's analogical comparison.

Malcolm uses Job as an example to show how God's actions do not heed to justification or explanation.[10] Job has come under terrible suffering; his livestock, family, home and health have been taken away from him. Job's friends then attempt to explain the reasons for his calamity and suffering: 'Who being innocent, has ever perished? Where were the upright destroyed? As I have observed, those who plough evil and those who sow trouble reap it.'[11] The explanation is simple: Job has sinned, and consequently he is being punished. Yet Job is not taken by this explanation, and says to his friends, 'Your maxims are proverbs of ashes; and your defences are defences of clay,'[12] 'How can you console me with your nonsense? Nothing is left of your answers but falsehood!'[13] Job realizes that his friends' explanations are simplistic, that indeed, there is no explanation; it is simply in the hands of God and Job can only utter, 'I put my hand over my mouth.'[14] There is still the suffering that is as real after their explanations as before. Causal explanations and theories do not hold the religious significance of the simple statement, 'It is the will of God.'

In contrast to Job's friends' search for explanations, Malcolm observes:

> It is pointless to continue seeking for an explanation. We are faced with a fact which we must *accept*. 'That's how it is!' The words, 'It is God's will', have many religious connotations: but they also have a logical force similar to 'That's how it is!' Both expressions tell us to stop asking 'Why' and instead to *accept a fact!*[15]

He sees a tie between the religious believer's remark 'It is the will of God', which would also include, 'I put my hand over my mouth', and Wittgenstein's agitation at excessive philosophical explanation; both see the inability of explanations to elucidate the examples of religious expressions and philosophical problems. Furthermore, explanations may possibly mislead one into erroneous conclusions, such as assuming that the religious believer must have a rational justification for God allowing children to suffer, or that the philosopher must be able to deductively conclude, with the method of logical atomism, for instance, the meaning of a proposition. The point here is not that there is *no* explanation, but that explanations come to an end. There comes a point where we simply accept that the word 'five', as in Wittgenstein's shopkeeper example, is used in an accepted manner, where what is required is not the Tractarian connection to names and simple objects, but a connection to our ordinary language. In other words, the explanation is found in the way we use language, not in working out the logical syntax of a proposition down to a simple object. Likewise, when Job says, in effect, that it is in the hands of God, this is not an explanation for his suffering, but a response to it. We do not need an explanation for our use of the word 'five', or for God's actions. Rather, we use the word 'five' and the statement 'It is the will of God' within the language-game of counting and religion, respectively.

Malcolm notes that the 'assumption that *everything* can be explained filled Wittgenstein with a kind of fury'.[16] As Wittgenstein notes: 'Giving grounds, however justifying the evidence, comes to an end; – but the end is not certain propositions' striking us immediately as true, i.e. it is not a kind of *seeing* on our part; it is our *acting*, which lies at the bottom of the language-game.'[17] Hence, the end of explanation is, according to Malcolm, to be understood in the light of the language-game which does not need further qualification and explanation, but is sufficient itself.[18] Language-games do not depend on a logical syntax underlying them in order to have a meaning, just as the believer does not feel satisfied saying, 'It is the will of God', because of the logical explanations that can be deduced from the statement; rather, the force of the proposition lies in its contextual surroundings of language in use. Malcolm comments:

> Wittgenstein regarded language-games, and their associated forms of life, as beyond explanation. The inescapable logic of this conception is that the terms 'explanation,' 'reason,' 'justification,' have a use *exclusively within* the various language-games. The word 'explanation' appears in many different language-games, and is used differently in different games ... An explanation is *internal* to a particular language-game. There is no explanation that *rises above* our language-games, and explains *them*. This would be a *super-concept* of explanation – which means that it is an ill-conceived fantasy.[19]

Just as our explanations cannot rise above God to explain the tragedies in life, so our explanations cannot rise above the language-games. Rather than ratiocination, we need only, according to Malcolm, look at the facts of the situation and describe them, not explain them away. When we 'make a particular study of a language-game [then we] can say to someone: "Look at it! That's how it is! Don't ask why, but take it as a fact, without explanation!" We need to *accept* the everyday language game',[20] just as Job accepts the will of God.

For example, we do not take the fact that there is a tree in front of us to be correct only when we are satisfied with the truth of the matter through rigorous explanation. As Wittgenstein writes, 'I did not get my picture of the world by satisfying myself of its correctness; nor do I have it because I am satisfied of its correctness. No: it is the inherited background against which I distinguish between true and false.'[21] In other words, we do not *know* the truth of the proposition that there is a tree in front of us; rather, the proposition that there is a tree in front of us need not accept any doubt or proof. Moreover, Wittgenstein states:

I do not explicitly learn the propositions that stand fast for me. I can *discover* them subsequently like the axis around which a body rotates. This axis is not fixed in the sense that anything holds it fast, but the movement around it determines its immobility.[22]

It is interesting to note the difference between Wittgenstein's conception and that of Shields, for whom there is a fixed base that holds all fast, namely God and the pre-established conditions, and the movement around this fixed base is, conversely, determined by that which holds all fast. While Wittgenstein's later thought becomes quite radical, Shields, for example, wants to continue the foundational understanding of building upon a fixed and pre-existent horizon which determines all that revolves around it. Remember that Shields states, 'without "God", understood in the sense of a binding horizon, expressions would mean whatever anyone wanted them to mean, and each interpretation would be neither better nor worse than another'.[23] Shields thinks he is firmly grounding language – removing doubt and relativism – but is his method really necessary?

If we were to doubt propositions that stand fast, then it is not so much the case that we are properly investigating the matter to find the ground, but that we would be crazy.[24] What if we tried to prove that the tree in front of us was not in front of us, or if I tried to prove that I have not been typing at my computer? Just as it is crazy to try to prove that these things are not the case, it is equally absurd to try to prove that they are the case. Wittgenstein illustrates: 'My difficulty can also be shown like this: I am sitting talking to a friend. Suddenly I say: "I knew all along that you were so-and-so." ... I feel as if these words were like "good morning" said to someone in the middle of a conversation.'[25] Similarly, we do not say to our friend sitting on a bench with us that we know the bench beneath us exists, nor do we say that we know God's reasoning, plans and thoughts. There is a similarity between the limit of explanations in Wittgenstein's philosophy and, according to Malcolm, a religious viewpoint: just as Job accepts God's actions without explanation, language-games are accepted as descriptions, not as something to be determined and proved as true or to be doubted – which can lead to vacuous expressions such as, 'I know I am now typing.' There is a point at which explanations stop and we say with Wittgenstein, 'I have reached bedrock, and my spade is turned.'[26]

Malcolm points out the significance of the limit of explanation – the point at which the spade is turned – in the context of the inclination to be amazed at the existence of the language-games and the world. Wittgenstein says, 'I wonder at the existence of the world', and this is 'seeing the world as a miracle'.[27] This is not simply a questioning of the empirical process involved in the creation of the world, as if one's wonder can be quenched by the presentation of the explanation for the existence of the world; instead, it is simply a wonder that the world exists.

Just as there is a wonder at the existence of the world, there is also a wonder at the existence of language-games. Wittgenstein remarks: 'Let yourself be *struck* by the existence of such a thing as our language-game.'[28] The existence of the world and the language-games are outside the domain of explanation; they simply exist.[29] We can see how this fits with the cornerstone of Malcolm's analogies that there is a limit to explanation: since the world and language-games cannot be explained, it then follows that they can only be described. There is an unquestionable authority in both Wittgenstein's later understanding of language and a 'religious point of view', namely, the language-games and the will of God. Their authority is not derived from an explanation; rather, it is accepted. Wittgenstein writes: 'Believing means submitting to an authority.'[30]

Malcolm, however, realizes that the problem of excessive explanations and theorizing is not easily stopped, and he relates the problem of not heeding to the limit of explanation to an illness.[31] Indeed, Wittgenstein notes: 'Our illness is this, to want to explain.'[32] In particular, it is the illness of not stopping at descriptions, and instead 'yielding to the temptation to explain everyday actions, reactions, abilities, by inventing "reservoirs" of mental states, intermediary steps, underlying mechanisms'.[33] These problematic confusions are not limited to a few philosophers. Rather, Wittgenstein regards the discipline of philosophy to be replete with problems: 'philosophy isn't anything except philosophical problems'.[34] Moreover, he realizes the difficulty within himself: 'how hard I find it to see what is *right in front of my eyes*!'[35] Thus, a 'philosopher is a man who has to cure many intellectual diseases in himself before he can arrive at the notions of common sense'.[36] Philosophical confusion is a continual struggle not only within the field of philosophy, but also within oneself.

Malcolm compares illness within a philosophical context to illness within a religious context. For example, fears, hatred, lack of morality, etc. are understood within a religious point of view as a fault in the human condition – we are not intrinsically good.[37] And Wittgenstein notes, 'people are religious in the degree that they believe themselves to be not so much *imperfect* as *ill*'.[38] Illness, in the religious sense, is manifested in the temptation towards immoral behaviour, while illness in philosophy is illustrated by the temptation towards excessive explanations (i.e. to think that there is, or at least will be, an answer to each and every problem). In philosophical and religious contexts, illness is a deep-seated condition that is not to be taken lightly, and needs to be remedied.

As noted previously, Wittgenstein says, 'the philosopher's treatment of a question is like the treatment of an illness'.[39] The therapy for the illness of philosophical confusion is not to investigate deeper and deeper for a solution but, once again, to turn our spade. Wittgenstein notes:

> a remarkable and characteristic phenomena in philosophical investi-gation: the difficulty – I might say – is not that of finding the solution but rather of recognizing as the solution something that looks as if it were only a preliminary to it ... This is connected, I believe, with our wrongly expecting an explanation, whereas the solution of the diffi-culty is a description, if we give it the right place in our considerations. If we dwell upon it, and do not try to get beyond it. The difficultly here is: to stop.[40]

Stopping the continual search for explanations is not perfunctory; rather, it points to the importance of describing the applications of language. Wittgenstein is not concerned with empirical explanations; rather, he says 'we must do away with all explanation and description must take its place'.[41] What is of primary importance is to stop the misguided attempt to dig beneath the bedrock, and instead observe the concrete practices that speak for themselves.[42] The 'therapeutic' aspect of Wittgenstein's later philosophy points to the primacy of doing and acting over intellectualizing.[43]

The primacy of doing and acting in Wittgenstein's later philosophy finds, according to Malcolm, an analogue in religion. He notes that Wittgenstein would have agreed with St James that 'faith without works is dead'.[44] In a religious context it is the lifestyle (religious practices) of the believer that is primary in contrast, for example, to speculative theories for the proof of God's existence.[45] Similarly, Wittgenstein's later understanding of language places human action and reaction within the language-games as primary, in contrast to philosophical theorizing. Just as the language-game is based in activities – 'it is our *acting*, which lies at the bottom of the language game'[46] – so in religion practices take precedence over theorizing.

Wittgenstein says he 'sees every problem from a religious point of view', and the question of what relation there could be between his philosophy and religion is an interesting and serious one. Malcolm discusses this relation by comparing Wittgenstein's later conception of language and philosophy to a 'religious point of view'. For example, not paying attention to the limit of explanation is a type of illness (philosophical confusion) that needs to be treated by turning one's viewpoint back to the activities of the language-games. Similarly, within a religious context there is a limit of explanation for God's will, and there is no theory that demonstrates the nature of God. However, religious practices show an understanding of God and the importance of living according to God's will. Malcolm clearly shows an interesting relationship between Wittgenstein's later philosophy and a 'religious point of view' while maintaining his original stance that there is something analogous to a religious point of view, not something that is strictly a religious point of view.[47]

The problem of equating philosophy and religion and the importance of religious examples

Malcolm's discussion of the relation between Wittgenstein's later philosophy and a 'religious point of view' is helpful since he clearly shows an understanding of Wittgenstein's later philosophy and does not confuse it with religion. One weakness, however, is Malcolm's lack of concrete religious examples. Yet this omission is not integral to Malcolm's work; consequently, the use of specific religious terms (e.g. Hebraic thought) to better illuminate the religious nature of an analogy does not conflict with his work. William DeAngelis, however, provides an illustration of the problems of conflating philosophy with religion and of actively denying the value of specific religious examples. These two problems represent the exact opposite approach taken by this study; namely, to keep religion and philosophy distinct, and to use a specific religious example to further clarify the analogy between Wittgenstein's later philosophy and a religious point of view.

DeAngelis thinks Malcolm's discussion of illness, in particular, is the solution to the question of what Wittgenstein's religious point of view is. He states:

> I think that he [Malcolm] is right in suggesting that Wittgenstein would have seen this feature of his late philosophical writings [the need to change one's life to cure diseases of thought] as representative of a religious point of view. As such, I accept Malcolm's third analogy as a modest, partial solution to his book's central problem.[48]

Malcolm, however, keeps philosophy and religion distinct; and in particular notes that his third analogy cannot be understood as equating religious illness with philosophical illness.[49] Nevertheless, DeAngelis, writes:

> Malcolm asserts that Wittgenstein's late approach to philosophy is analogous to a religious approach to the problems of life. My remarks ... suggest a stronger connection between the two: namely, that the former is not merely *analogous to* but is *an instance of* the latter.[50]

DeAngelis goes much further than Malcolm and boldly claims that Wittgenstein's thought *is* religious as it stands.

As noted in the previous chapter, Shields relates philosophical problems to religion, and in particular to sin. Both Shields and DeAngelis give philosophy a religious ethic, in the sense that doing philosophy with the goal of clarity is considered religious. Despite this similarity, the two approach the association of religion with philosophy very differently. Shields defines his use of religion as based on the Reformed tradition and with a particular emphasis on sin, while DeAngelis uses religion as a blanket term to cover the idea of approaching life with the attitude to better oneself and fix the problems of thought. In effect, Shields keeps the analogy with religion (however inappropriate it may be) by comparing a religious point (the Reformed tradition and sin) with Wittgenstein's philosophy, whereas DeAngelis's effort is weakened by giving no particular religious application.

DeAngelis is not discussing sin, nor is he discussing any spiritual illness of religious people (such as Shields's example of Augustine); rather, he is discussing only the philosophical attitude of wanting to improve oneself and to clarify problems of thought. DeAngelis considers the desire to seek clarity, and to thereby rid onself of the illness of unclarity, to be religious.[51] Unlike the previous discussion of Shields, which looked at the Reformed tradition and sin as applied to Wittgenstein's philosophy, we have no such case example to look at in DeAngelis's work. Hence, rather than showing that a particular religious analogy has potential problems when related to Wittgenstein's thought, we now need to look at the problems associated with not giving any particular examples from religion and at the same time maintaining that Wittgenstein's philosophy is religious.

Since DeAngelis's definition of 'religious' is limited to an approach that seeks clarity and knows that the problem of confusion resides within oneself,[52] it is difficult to understand the religious application of his definition without further substantiation. The point here is not that DeAngelis's conception of clarity as religious is a contradiction to religion, but rather to ask what the religious application is? Saying, for example, that honouring one's parents is a religious attitude, although this may be true (it is the fourth commandment), adds nothing to the discussion since it is also the attitude for many non-religious people as well. It may be part of a religious viewpoint, and Wittgenstein might have said that it is good to honour one's parents, but in and of itself it is difficult to understand as a significant religious point, unless all irreligious people dishonour their parents. To want to honour one's parents, or to want to change one's life to clarify philosophical problems, could be called religious, but these are not effective analogies with which we can definitively say that Wittgenstein's philosophy *is* religious. Just as an analogy of wooden bookcases and desks can be drawn on the basis that they are composed of wood, but the analogy offers little detail since many things are composed of wood. All that is being offered by DeAngelis's point is a general notion that improvement is a good thing, but if this is all a religious viewpoint has to offer, then why even discuss it? It would be quite unusual to find a particular area of thought, be it philosophical, religious, unphilosophical or irreligious, in which improvement is considered as something to be avoided. Granted, there may be different ideas of what improvement amounts to, but in each case it is improvement, nonetheless, that is sought. Also, it is very unlikely that people from any one viewpoint would think that their particular thought, when improved, leads to further confusion.

It is not, however, a mistake that DeAngelis draws upon no religious examples of practices, creeds or mythologies. He comes to the conclusion that there is no need to discuss a religious example since all particular religious distinctions (which would actually give more meaning and understanding to the analogy made) are to be overlooked. Rather than seeing the lack of meaning and context in his conception of the religious as a weakness, he thinks it is a strength: 'There is no requirement that this attitude connect with the practices or theological doctrines of any established religion. ... the absence of any such requirement is clearly not an oversight.'[53] Moreover,

> Wittgenstein saw no need for such qualifications. His thought was that the attitude described in the passage is religious, whether or not it is connected with conventional religious practices or dogmas. Indeed, he seemed to think that this attitude is more purely religious when it has no such connections.[54]

DeAngelis is correct to point out that there are no explicit references to a particular religion in Wittgenstein's writings in general, and that there is no need to attach a 'religious' attitude, but his conclusion that Wittgenstein therefore considers religious practices as unnecessary trappings is highly questionable. According to DeAngelis, we are 'more purely religious' without connections to religious traditions and practices; consequently, 'conventional mythologies or theological concepts are not necessary for genuine faith, and that when they function to reinforce it, it can be a sign of weak faith'.[55] Indeed, conventional mythologies and concepts are not necessarily required, but surely DeAngelis's point is not that *un*conventional mythologies and concepts are better. Instead, he denounces mythologies and concepts entirely in order to be 'more purely religious'. This is a very odd conception of the term 'religious'.

Consider an example of the importance of context. The term 'sportsman-like' means that a person plays a particular sport fairly, whereas unsportsman-like conduct is to play unfairly and cheat. Now if we wanted, we could take the meaning of this term out of the sport context and say that someone is sportsman-like to mean only that they deal fairly with others. However, we would have no idea of what the term means without reference to sport, and more importantly, could we say that a person is more 'purely' sportsman-like by removing all connections to sport? Do football players show that they have a weak sportsman-like attitude through using traditional understandings of the rules of the game? It would be difficult, if not impossible, to say that we are more sportsman-like by removing ourselves as far as possible from the tradition and practices within sport. It would be quite odd to say 'Smith plays with true sportsman-like conduct', and then, when asked why this is, offer no example (such as saying, 'He never pushes other players offside') and say, 'He simply has a sportsman-like approach which is best understood without any reference to the game.' Likewise, how can we better understand the term 'religious' without looking to the application of religious practices? It is important to note that this does not imply that the term 'religious' applies to one particular religion or practice; just as sportsman-like does not apply to one sport, we cannot reduce religion to practices, but both terms are better understood through examples from religion or sport. Granted, cross-over uses can occur in everyday conversations, but to say, as DeAngelis does, that the 'pure' use of the term is to be removed entirely from the context in which the term holds its meaning is very questionable.

Nevertheless, DeAngelis approvingly quotes Engelmann's remark as further evidence of not paying attention to specific practices or mythologies:

> The person who had achieved this insight – 'I shall never find a way out of the chaos of my emotions and thoughts so long as I have not achieved the supreme and crucial insight that that discrepancy is not the fault of life as it is, but myself as I am.' – and holds onto it, and who will at least try again and again throughout his life to live up to it, is religious. He has the faith, from which it does not follow by any means that he must use mythological concepts – self created or handed down – to buttress and interpret his insight into the fundamental relationship between himself and human existence in general. If he depends on such concepts in order to stand by his faith, the reason may well lie in a weakness of faith. He should be able to stand by it without justification or explanation.[56]

Engelmann is right to note that the faults in life are not simply a problem
with life itself, but are within oneself, and he is also correct to note that
there is no need of religious concepts to capture this idea. Moreover, he is
right to maintain that the religious person need not seek justification and
explanations for their faith through religion. The problem, however, is
that although Engelmann rightly rejects the use of mythological concepts
to justify one's faith, he indirectly dismisses the significance of the mythological in religion. He thinks that the one who sees the problems in life as
a personal issue, instead of a problem of life itself, 'is religious' and 'has the
faith'. Why call this understanding 'the faith' or 'religious'? Engelmann's
description of 'the fault of life being within oneself' can equally be applied
to a materialist atheist (or do all atheists think that the problems of life
reside with life itself and not the individual?). Nevertheless, Engelmann
says that the person who realizes that the problems with life are within
oneself *is* religious.[57] To use the term 'religious' in describing an understanding that the fault of life resides within oneself is acceptable, but to say
simply on this basis alone that such a person *is* religious is questionable.
Are we to call the atheist who believes the fault of life is within oneself
'religious'? DeAngelis's and Engelmann's points are arguable, but when
they label their perspectives as 'religious' (without further substantiation)
they may be conflating a philosophical point with religion.

The problem of disregarding particular practices and associations for
the term 'religious' can be seen as similar to the following: if we are asked
why Jones is musical, then we might say 'Jones is musical because he can
sing', but this would be using a conventional understanding of what being
musical is (i.e. singing). It would be peculiar if we said there need not
be any reference to music at all; indeed, the 'purely' musical person has
nothing to do with the tradition or practice of music. If this is really what
we hold, then we would no longer be discussing music. Moreover, why
would we still want to use the word 'musical'? Surely, DeAngelis would
not hold this view of a person with a musical nature, but he seems to hold
this type of understanding for a person with a religious nature. This is
the sort of confusion we end up in if a religious point of view is abstracted
from its context and pared of its practice.[58] It is true that one can decide
not to use the religious category, can dismiss traditional mythologies and
concepts, and can see the confusion in explanations and justifications for
religion, but why bring the term 'religious' back if we are intentionally not

discussing religion? To use musical or religious concepts is not necessarily to justify being musical or religious; rather, it is the language-game of music and religion.

In the light of Wittgenstein's emphasis on the application and practice associated with language, can it be said, as DeAngelis has indicated, that Wittgenstein regards the best discussion of religion to exclude: qualifications, doctrines, established religions and religious practices?[59] And can we say that Wittgenstein thought a discussion of religion that excludes these factors is more 'purely religious?'[60] Granted, it is true that Wittgenstein may not have actually subscribed to a particular religious practice or creed, so to speak, but that does not mean we can better understand religion without looking at the associated practice and creed. In other words, we need not practise a religion to discuss religion, but it is helpful to describe a practice when discussing religion. Nevertheless, DeAngelis thinks that Wittgenstein expresses a religious viewpoint, but does not explicitly discuss a particular religion; therefore, he thinks such specific narrowness is unnecessary, and perhaps better done without.

Yet cannot we draw another conclusion, namely that Wittgenstein was not attempting to equate religion and philosophy in his writings at all. In other words, the lack of particular 'religious' claims is not evidence for knowingly thinking them to be unimportant; rather, they may have nothing at all to do with the work at hand. DeAngelis's first error is to think that Wittgenstein is equating philosophy and religion, which then leads to his second error, to assume that since there are no examples of a particular religion in Wittgenstein's writing, religion is best discussed without specific examples. We would never say, 'Since Augustine does not discuss the details of the variety of pears he stole, such details are not important when discussing horticulture.' DeAngelis, nevertheless, thinks that since Wittgenstein does not explicitly discuss any one religion, such discussion is irrelevant when discussing religion. This leaves the reigns of practice and theology – the grammar of religion – behind in pursuit of the 'pure' religious attitude.

Since DeAngelis does not use any particular religious examples, he easily equates the philosophical attitude to clarify thought and to realize the problems in oneself with a religious attitude. It then follows that there must be a direct correlation between philosophical clarity and one's religious nature. Wittgenstein, however, would never allow such a direct correlation of mutually gained appreciation between philosophy and religion. Indeed, as philosophical problems become clarified, a person could just as easily turn away from a religious point of view. Wittgenstein says 'new language-games ... come into existence, and others become obsolete and are forgotten',[61] so it is possible that a particular religious practice (language-game) loses all significance for a person. It is possible that as philosophical clarity is gained, a religious viewpoint is lost (or vice versa). This raises an interesting point: if the language-game of a religion is defunct for an individual, then that religious point of view would be obsolete for that individual. However, DeAngelis would then consider the individual to be approaching the 'pure' religious point of view. To reiterate his point:

> Wittgenstein saw no need for such qualifications. His thought was that the attitude described in the passage is religious, whether or not it is connected with conventional religious practices or dogmas. Indeed, he seemed to think that this attitude is more purely religious when it has no such connections.[62]

This creates an odd incongruity: if someone loses their religious point of view, say as a Hindu, and no longer holds any thoughts or practices associated with Hinduism, or any other religion, then DeAngelis would say (as long as the person still wants to clarify their thoughts) this person is finally gaining a 'pure' religious attitude. Yet it seems just as plausible to say that this person now has *no* religious point of view at all.

Since DeAngelis does not emphasize practice (i.e. he considers the move from religious practices to be a move toward the more 'purely' religious), he misses the significance of the practice associated with the language-games. Indeed, DeAngelis takes no interest in the practices of the language-game of any religion, which could help clarify what a religious point of view could be; instead, he is interested in abstract notions of improvement. He disregards religious examples entirely and calls the aim for clarity in philosophy religious.[63] Consequently, his work provides an example of the problems of conflating religion and philosophy and missing the significance and distinct nature of religious examples.

Towards a concrete discussion of a religious analogy

Malcolm's discussion of Wittgenstein's 'religious point of view' observes interesting similarities between Wittgenstein's later thought and a 'religious point of view'. Malcolm understands that there is a difference between philosophy and religion throughout his study and simply draws a general analogical relation between the two. Moreover, Malcolm's intriguing question – what is Wittgenstein's 'religious point of view'? – deserves further reflection. Wittgenstein does say he cannot help seeing every problem from a religious point of view. Yet Malcolm writes: 'Do these analogies present the meaning of Wittgenstein's remark that he saw philosophical problems from a religious point of view? I do not know. I cannot answer with any confidence.'[64] Malcolm's task is inherently difficult. Winch, nevertheless, endeavours to understand Wittgenstein's religious point of view through a discussion of his letter to Drury. Winch wants to show that Wittgenstein's attitude to philosophical problems is similar to his attitude in dealing with Drury's problem.[65] In other words, the attitude with which Wittgenstein tackles philosophical problems is similar to the attitude shown in Wittgenstein's letter to Drury.

When Drury was in his first residency as a physician, he told Wittgenstein he was 'distressed' at his 'own ignorance and clumsiness', and Wittgenstein simply told Drury that it was a matter of lacking experience.[66] Wittgenstein, however, sent Drury a letter of understanding the next day:

> Don't think about yourself, but think of others ... You said in the park yesterday that possibly you had made a mistake in taking up medicine: you immediately added that probably it was wrong to think such a thing at all. I am sure it is. But not because being a doctor you may not go the wrong way, or go to the dogs, but because if you do, this has nothing to do with the choice of profession being a mistake. For what human being can say what would have been the right thing if this is the wrong one? You didn't make a mistake because there was nothing at the time you knew or ought to have known that you overlooked. Only this one could have called making a mistake: and even if you had made a mistake in this sense, this would now have to be regarded as a datum as all other circumstances inside and outside which you can't

alter (control). The thing now is to live in the world in which you are, not to think or dream about the world you would like to be in. Look at people's sufferings, physical and mental, you have them close at hand, and this ought to be a good remedy for your troubles. Another way is to take a rest whenever you ought to take one and collect yourself ... As to religious thoughts I do not think the craving for placidity is religious: I think a religious person regards placidity or peace as a gift from heaven, not something one ought to hunt after. Look at your patients more closely as human beings in trouble and enjoy the opportunity you have to say 'good night' to so many people. This alone is a gift from heaven which many people would envy you. And this sort of thing ought to heal your frayed soul, I believe. It won't rest it; but when you are healthily tired you can just take a rest. I think in some sense you don't look at people's faces closely enough.[67]

According to Winch, Wittgenstein's letter is concerned with Drury's '*spiritual welfare*' and 'clearly expresses the quasi-religious idea that life imposes certain duties on us' by offering a 'major *philosophical* point' (philosophical confusion) discussed in an 'overall quasi-religious concern for Drury's spiritual health'.[68] The letter is, according to Winch, 'infused with religious sensibility'.[69] It is correct to note a religious aspect in Wittgenstein's letter, but it is difficult to grasp Winch's point here regarding the 'religious sensibility' and the 'quasi-religious' nature of a philosophical point.

Presumably the point Wittgenstein does show, in his letter to Drury, is that it is not a mistake for Drury to be in the medical profession, that instead he should take it as a gift, look at his surroundings, and act and react to his employment. This is linked to the 'religious' claim Wittgenstein makes, that 'placidity' is a 'gift from heaven' rather than something we can capture. As Winch wants to show, this can be seen as similar to Wittgenstein's approach to philosophical confusion, in which case we must look at the language-game that is played instead of thinking that it is all a mistake (doubt), or that there is something behind it (underlying structures). Instead we must look at the language-game and accept it, just as we must accept our vocation and do our best instead of looking for explanations to convince ourselves that it is the right occupation. For Wittgenstein, hunting for 'placidity' is similar to hunting for excessive explanations in philosophy, both of which lead either to despair or to confusion.

Wittgenstein's advice, however, does not seem to have any particular religious attachment. It is good advice and shows a genuine concern for Drury, but there is no distinctive religious application with which to better understand Wittgenstein's possible religious point of view. Hence, Winch uses the term 'quasi-religious', but such a term is vague and unhelpful. The first thing to ask is, 'What is religious?' and then 'What is "quasi-religious?"' To answer the first question, we would need to look at religion – which is not done – and then for the second question, we need to see what seems to be religious in our example (Wittgenstein's letter), but this is very difficult if we have not shown what is religious in the first instance.

Winch's effort to understand Wittgenstein's religious point of view is similar to Malcolm's own attempt since he and Winch do not discuss a concrete religious example. Hence, Winch adds the term 'quasi-religious' to his discussion, fully understanding that his attempt is a 'very sketchy' way to better understand Wittgenstein's remark.[70] Moreover, Winch describes his use of the term religious as 'elusive'.[71] It is not surprising, then, that Winch makes a remark similar to that of Malcolm regarding his project: 'The perspective I have tried to sketch in this last section offers a much less clear-cut interpretation than do Malcolm's 'analogies' of what he [Wittgenstein] meant in the remark to Drury.'[72] Even if we say that, in his remark to Drury, Wittgenstein is referring to a sense of gratitude, that there is a sense of gratitude in a religious perspective, it does not follow that it is a religious perspective or a quasi-religious perspective any more than it is a Humanistic perspective or a quasi-Humanistic perspective. Perhaps we can say, without blunder, that there is a sense of gratitude in a religious perspective, but there is a sense of gratitude in many perspectives, and it does not make the discussion any more concrete.

Wittgenstein's letter to Drury can be seen as an initiation into discussing his religious point of view, but on its own does not really demonstrate what the point of view is. Winch notes this difficulty: 'This brings into focus a point which would anyway have to be faced, namely that there is much unclarity concerning the kind of terms we should use in distinguishing between a "religious" and a "non-religious" point of view.'[73] Winch says that even he, like Malcolm, is not certain of the best way to proceed with Wittgenstein' remark:

> I am grateful to Norman Malcolm, as for so much else, for making me think about the whole issue in a way I should probably not otherwise have come to. Of course he himself explicitly disclaimed any pretension to finality or certainty in his interpretation. And I want to make the same sort of disclaimer.[74]

Winch does, however, offer a seed to understanding:

> However, as far as we are concerned the position is not hopeless. We are not in the business of trying to arrive at a definition, or even a characterization, of a religious belief that would cover all cases. We need only consider the forms of religious belief towards which Wittgenstein himself was most sympathetic or felt himself most inclined.[75]

This is a valuable path to follow; it is very important to understand what Wittgenstein might have meant by a religious point of view. Winch's and Malcolm's discussions of Wittgenstein's 'religious point of view' are insightful, and they profitably lead to further investigation into a concrete analogy for his 'religious point of view'. They do not, however, offer a concrete understanding of a religious point of view to clarify the discussion. Consequently, their discussions are rather indeterminate, or as Winch says, 'sketchy'.

Winch notes, 'if we want to understand the way in which a system of ideas is related to reality, we had best proceed by examining the actual application in life of those ideas rather than, as it were, fastening our attention on the peculiar nature of "entities referred to" by them'.[76] The terms 'wonder', 'marvel', 'illness' and 'spiritual welfare' all leave a feeling of generality. Winch seems to think that these words are not simply religious when discussing Wittgenstein, but they are quasi-religious. The question raised, of course, is how does a practice relate to the quasi-religious, or for that matter to the quasi-ethical or quasi-aesthetical? Wittgenstein's statement in *On Certainty* seems to apply here, namely, 'all psychological terms merely lead us away from the main thing'.[77] The implication is that we need not look harder for the right word, but realize that we are looking in the wrong direction. We need to look at the application of religious terms, not some type of common attitude that could be religious, or quasi-religious; just as when discussing logic Wittgenstein says that all we can do is look at the practice of language, then we see logic, while to discuss logic through any other manner, including psychological terms, only leads to confusion.[78]

Despite the lack of particular examples in his discussion of Wittgenstein's remark, Winch does realize the most appropriate way to proceed: 'it would seem natural for us to raise the question of what particular sort of religion, or religious belief he [Wittgenstein] has in mind'.[79] But instead of following through, he stops and posits the quasi-religious. Part of the reason for not seeking specific religious viewpoints is a commonly accepted point, namely, when discussing Wittgenstein and religion, it is not easy to locate Wittgenstein within any one religious tradition. It is well known that Wittgenstein did not follow a particular religious practice. Hence, according to Winch, 'the phrase "from a religious point of view" cannot be interpreted in terms of any particular theological doctrine'.[80] And as Drury states regarding Wittgenstein:

> For Pascal there was only one true religion, Christianity: only one true form of Christianity, Catholicism; only one true expression of Catholicism, Port Royal. Now although Wittgenstein would have respected this narrowness for its very intensity, such exclusiveness was foreign to his way of thinking.[81]

And as Wittgenstein remarks, 'the way in which people have had to express their religious beliefs differ enormously. All genuine expressions of religion are wonderful even those of the most savage peoples.'[82] Moreover, Wittgenstein says that he is not religious.[83] Although all these statements can show that Wittgenstein did not subscribe to a particular religious point of view, they do not show that he does not have a better understanding of one religious point of view over another. Surely, one's footing, even if one is not an adherent to a particular religion, is best found in the background in which they live.

If we are going to say that it is necessary to look at the application in order to understand religion, then it is also necessary to understand the context of Wittgenstein's remarks regarding religion and, as Winch states, his inclinations[84] – unless we assume that Wittgenstein understood the one universal religion – the 'pure' religion – or, in other words, unless we assume that all religions are basically the same. Certainly Wittgenstein's remark that he cannot help but see every problem from a religious point of view does not mean *the one absolute* religious point of view (as if all the differences in the various religions are irrelevant), but from *a* religious point of view. Accordingly, it seems in such an instance that the most appropriate place to look is Wittgenstein's own inclinations – his footing – in order to understand what he may mean by a religious point of view.

An objection may be raised here: when Wittgenstein speaks of a religious point of view, it is, of course, a style of thinking not to be related to any one religion. But what, then, is the point of the remark? The reply may be that there is a sense of the religious in Wittgenstein's thought, but what religious sense? The answer is likely to be, of course, the spiritual concern for others, the limit of explanation, etc. However, as stated previously, this implies the presupposition that all religions equally hold these sorts of ideas, which is similar to saying that all ethical practices are the same because they seek the good.

The point here is that, although a generalization could perhaps be made regarding a religious point of view, there is admittedly a spiritual concern for others, etc., the actual practice may in fact work out quite differently between religions. Once we drop the particulars, we are left with a vague generalization that can apply over a broad range of subjects, which then weakens the analogy. This is an important point since it is not the case that analogies must fit one hundred per cent – in which case there is no point to the analogy – yet there must be points of contact between an analogy and its application. Wittgenstein notes that we can run into difficulties trying to find a definition for ethics, and that 'in such a difficulty always ask yourself: How did we learn the meaning of this word ("good" for instance)? Then it will be easier for you to see that the word must have a family of meanings.'[85] Likewise, if we discuss a religious analogy, then it is helpful to look at its religious application in order to grasp its meaning. There must be more to religious analogies than simply thinking that improvement is a good thing, and that the fault of life is within oneself, are *ipso facto* religious (unless we are going to say that only religious people seek improvement and realize the problems within themselves, while non-religious people seek degeneration and think all problems reside in others). To purposefully reject specific religious contexts in order to understand the meaning of being religious leads to confusion instead of clarity, and it goes against the grain of Wittgenstein's later thought.

The clarification of Wittgenstein's philosophy and a 'religious point of view'

Malcolm provides an illuminating discussion that contributes to our understanding of the analogy between Wittgenstein's later philosophy and a 'religious point of view'. He correctly outlines the shift in Wittgenstein's thought from early to later and clearly places the latter as pivotal for a discussion of a 'religious point of view'. For example, a 'religious point of view' and Wittgenstein's later understanding of language similarly limit explanations; that is, neither God's will nor the language-games need explanations for their authority or meaning. Also, a 'religious point of view' and Wittgenstein's later conception of philosophy similarly treat the illness of excessive explanations by turning our attention to concrete practices within the form of life. For instance, in a religious context it is the turning around of one's life that is essential,[86] and in a philosophical context it is the description of language-game activities that is central. In both cases, religious and philosophical, *theories* do not explain meaning; rather, concrete practices show meaning.

Malcolm is careful, however, to keep the relation between philosophy and religion distinct. He emphasizes that he is discussing an analogy – not an equivalence.[87] Thus, he does not err, as Shields does, by saying Wittgenstein's philosophy *is* religious. The problem with Shields's approach is not only that he confounds philosophy and religion, he also chooses an inappropriate religious viewpoint (i.e. Calvinism and the Reformed tradition). Consequently, Shields confuses the discussion of Wittgenstein's philosophy and a religious point of view.

The right approach is not, however, to follow DeAngelis's method of purposefully disregarding the value of specific religious examples *in toto*. Rather, the best approach to clarify our understanding of the analogical relationship between Wittgenstein's later philosophy and a religious point of view, is to find a particular religious example that corresponds with the distinctive character of Wittgenstein's later philosophy and is applied only as an analogy. An awareness of these considerations offers a sound position to discern an appropriate and specific religious viewpoint that advances our understanding of the analogy between Wittgenstein's later philosophy and a 'religious point of view'.

Endnotes

1   Drury, 'Conversations with Wittgenstein', 79.
2   Malcolm, *Wittgenstein*, 1.
3   *Ibid.*, 24.
4   *Ibid.*, 3.
5   *Ibid.*, 38.
6   *Ibid.*, 3–4.
7   Malcolm, *Wittgenstein*, 92.
8   Wittgenstein, *Philosophical Investigations*, § 109.
9   *Ibid.*, § 126.
10 Malcolm, *Wittgenstein*, 3.
11 Job 4: 8–9.
12 *Ibid.*, 13: 12.
13 *Ibid.*, 21: 34.
14 *Ibid.*, 40: 4.
15 Malcolm, *Wittgenstein*, 86.
16 *Ibid.*, 85.
17 Wittgenstein, *On Certainty*, 204.
18 Malcolm, *Wittgenstein*, 86.
19 *Ibid.*, 77–8.
20 *Ibid.*, 86. See also Wittgenstein, *Philosophical Investigations*, p. 200.
21 Wittgenstein, *On Certainty*, 94.
22 *Ibid.*, 152.
23 Shields, *Logic and Sin*, 45.
24 Wittgenstein, *On Certainty*, 155.
25 *Ibid.*, 464.
26 Wittgenstein, *Philosophical Investigations*, § 217.
27 Ludwig Wittgenstein, 'Lecture on Ethics', *Philosophical Review*, 74 (January 1965), at 8, 11.
28 Wittgenstein, *Philosophical Investigations*, p. 224.

29 It is interesting to note, according to Abraham Heschel, that in Hebrew there is no word for doubt, but there are expressions for wonder. (96) Also, 'the cardinal question is not what is the law that would explain the interaction of phenomena in the universe, but why is there a law, a universe at all'. Abraham Joshua Heschel, *Between God and Man: An Interpretation of Judaism*, ed. Fritz A. Rothschild (New York: Harper Brothers, 1959), 100–1.

30 Wittgenstein, *Culture and Value*, 45e.

31 Malcolm, *Wittgenstein*, 92.

32 Ludwig Wittgenstein, *Remarks on the Foundations of Mathematics*, ed. G. H. von Wright, Rush Rhees and G. E. M. Anscombe, trans. G. E. M. Anscombe (Oxford: Basil Blackwell, 1978), 333.

33 Malcolm, *Wittgenstein*, 88.

34 Wittgenstein, *Philosophical Grammar*, 193.

35 Wittgenstein, *Culture and Value*, 39e.

36 *Ibid.*, 44e.

37 Malcolm, *Wittgenstein*, 87.

38 Wittgenstein, *Culture and Value*, 45e.

39 Wittgenstein, *Philosophical Investigations*, § 255.

40 Ludwig Wittgenstein, *Zettel*, ed. G. E. M. Anscombe and G. H. von Wright, trans. G. E. M. Anscombe (Oxford: Blackwell, 1967), 314.

41 Wittgenstein, *Philosophical Investigations*, § 109.

42 Wittgenstein, *On Certainty*, 139.

43 Malcolm, *Wittgenstein*, 92.

44 *Ibid.*, 90.

45 *Ibid.*

46 Wittgenstein, *On Certainty*, 204.

47 Malcolm, *Wittgenstein*, 1.

48 William James DeAngelis, 'Ludwig Wittgenstein – A Religious Point of View? Thoughts on Norman Malcolm's Last Philosophical Project', *Dialogue*, 36 (Fall 1997), 839.

49 Malcolm, *Wittgenstein*, 89.

50 DeAngelis, 'Ludwig Wittgenstein', 837.

51 *Ibid.*, 836.

52 *Ibid.*, 836–7.

53 *Ibid.*, 836.

54 *Ibid.*

55   *Ibid.*

56   Engelmann, *Letters From Wittgenstein*, 77.

57   Compare this with Rhees's comment on Wittgenstein and psycho-analysis: 'He sometimes spoke of analogies in *method*. The functional disorders which philosophy treats appear as delusions and dreams of our language.' Note that Rhees does not then say Wittgenstein *is* a psychoanalyst. Rhees, *Discussions of Wittgenstein*, 45.

58   Even if we say a person can be called musical simply because they appreciate music, with no actual musical practice or competency of their own, it is still, nevertheless, the musical practice they appreciate.

59   DeAngelis, 'Ludwig Wittgenstein', 836.

60   *Ibid.*

61   Wittgenstein, *Philosophical Investigations*, § 23.

62   DeAngelis, 'Ludwig Wittgenstein', 836.

63   When vague analogies are used it is easy to assume various religious backgrounds for Wittgenstein's thought. John V. Canfield, for example, says 'Wittgenstein's later philosophy and the doctrines of Mahayana Buddhism integral to Zen coincide in a fundamental aspect; for Wittgenstein language has, one might say, a mystical base; and this base is exactly the Buddhist ideal of acting with a mind empty of thought.' 'Wittgenstein and Zen', *Philosophy*, 50, 194 (October 1975), 383. This statement clearly does not appreciate differences, and conflates a vague conception of 'mystical' into an equivalence with Wittgenstein's understanding of language.

64   Malcolm, *Wittgenstein*, 92.

65   *Ibid.*, 125.

66   Drury, 'Conversations with Wittgenstein', 95.

67   *Ibid.*, 95–6.

68   Peter Winch, 'Discussion of Malcolm's Essay', in *Wittgenstein: A Religious Point of View?*, ed. P. Winch (New York: Cornell University Press, 1995), 126.

69   *Ibid.*

70   *Ibid.*, 124.

71   *Ibid.*, 132.

72   *Ibid.*

73   *Ibid.*, 109.

74   *Ibid.*, 132.

75   *Ibid.*, 109.

76   Peter Winch, *Trying to Make Sense* (Oxford: Basil Blackwell, 1987), 130.

77   Wittgenstein, *On Certainty*, 459.

78   *Ibid.*, 501.

79   Winch, 'Discussion of Malcolm's Essay', 108.

80   *Ibid.*

81   M. O'C. Drury, *The Danger of Words and Writings on Wittgenstein*, ed. David Berman, Michael Fitzgerald and John Hayes (Bristol: Thoemmes Press, 1996), 93.

82   Drury, 'Some Notes on Conversations', 93.

83   *Ibid.*, 79.

84   Winch, 'Discussion of Malcolm's Essay', 109.

85   Wittgenstein, *Philosophical Investigations*, § 77.

86   Wittgenstein says, 'I believe that one of the things Christianity says is that sound doctrines are all useless. That you have to change your life. (Or the direction of your life.).' Wittgenstein, *Culture and Value*, 53e.

87   Malcolm, *Wittgenstein*, 1.

3

Wittgenstein and Greek Thought

Concerning Wittgenstein's remark that he cannot help seeing every problem from a religious point of view, Shields and Malcolm question what his religious viewpoint could be. This is a relevant inquiry, as Winch notes: 'It would seem natural for us to raise the question of what particular sort of religion, or religious belief he [Wittgenstein] has in mind.'[1] The best response to this question is to take note of Wittgenstein's later philosophy and its focus on the concrete and practical, and then see if there is an analogical religious point of view. Moreover, the best way to understand a religious point of view is to discuss a specific religious point of view along with its religious terms and context. On the other hand, the direct correlation between the use of abstract terms and the positing of abstract objects they supposedly designate, leads attempts to interpret Wittgenstein's thought and a religious point of view from within an abstract paradigm to further confusion.

The contrast between abstract and foundational paradigms on the one hand, and Wittgenstein's later thought on the other, can be discussed in terms of Greek and Hebraic thought, respectively. The following discussion will show that Wittgenstein's later thought conflicts with Greek thought, while the fourth chapter will show that it is analogical to a particular strand of Hebraic thought. To contrast Greek and Hebraic thought in a comprehensive manner is, of course, beyond the scope of this discussion. Nevertheless, it is clear that Wittgenstein, in some sense, differentiates his Hebraic thought from Greek thought in his remark to Drury:

Of course it [Origen's idea][2] was rejected. It would make nonsense of everything else. If what we do now is to make no difference in the end, then all the seriousness of life is done away with. Your religious ideas have always seemed to me more Greek than biblical. Whereas my thoughts are one hundred percent Hebraic.[3]

The aspect of Greek thought that Wittgenstein refers to is set in the context of Origen's idea of re-establishment, which focuses upon a future spiritual realm that does not depend on our past or present activities.[4] In effect, our worldly life is inconsequential towards the end of re-establishment. Consequently, Origen's viewpoint can be read as devaluing the 'seriousness of life' by not counting our everyday activities as ultimately purposeful, whereas what is serious is the eventual re-establishment.

Origen's notion of an ideal beyond the world can be shown to be similar to, and perhaps influenced by, Plato. The ideal Forms of Plato are thought to hold absolute meaning and consequently inform our worldly lives, which are caught in the shadows of imperfect reflections of the ideal. Only by virtue of knowing ideal Beauty, for instance, can we come to know the imperfect beauty in the world. What is significant in this Greek aspect of thought is the positing of ideals beyond our everyday activities.

Even Wittgenstein, in his Tractarian work, exhibits an aspect of Greek thought (which will be shown as Platonic) in his discussion of language. Wittgenstein, in his early thought, overlooks the significance of our application of language in the world for meaning. He focuses on the underlying foundational logical structure of language – which is hidden by ordinary language – and the resultant analysis of the connection between names and the underlying simple objects. The aspect of Greek thought discussed, as applied to language, posits anchors for meaning outside our ordinary language and thereby removes the significance from our use of language in favour of an underlying logical structure and name-object relation. Wittgenstein's simple objects and Plato's Forms are abstractions.

The later Wittgenstein, however, as noted in the above remark to Drury, rejects this aspect of Greek thought. Wittgenstein's remark that the 'seriousness of life is done away with'[5] in Origen's thought corresponds with the idea that the seriousness of language use is 'done away with'. In both cases, our activities in life are not counted as significant towards the end of the re-establishment or meaning. Rather than dismissing the significance of practices and the applications of language in life, Wittgenstein dismisses the idea that there are significant and necessary anchors outside ordinary language to secure meaning. What becomes central for meaning in Wittgenstein's thought is the use of language within the language-games, that is, the forms of life.[6]

This important distinction between Greek thought and Wittgenstein's later thought is not based on a black and white notion of regarding the world and our activities as either futile or consequential; instead, the distinction rests on the idea that there must be something 'beyond', or other than, our mere actions and reactions within the world that informs or secures language and meaning. Wittgenstein, however, says 'don't think, but look!'[7] Wittgenstein will be shown to emphasize 'looking' (i.e. the description of the language-games we play), while Greek thought will be shown to emphasize 'thinking' (i.e. the unseen structure or Forms for language).

It is important to note that this is not a critique of the transcendent. There is no intent to reduce Wittgenstein's thought, the transcendent, the mind or religion, etc., to a materialistic mode. Wittgenstein's unsayable remains significant throughout his entire work, and the discussion is positively relating the Hebrew religion, which carries a notion of the transcendent, with Wittgenstein's thought. However, if the transcendent is thought to be a foundational support for language, which in turn is only a reflection or imitation of the transcendent, then the transcendent and language are misunderstood. Language does not gain meaning from the transcendent (the unsayable). Indeed, if we try to connect language to the transcendent (the unsayable) with the goal of security and meaning, we actually end up with confusion and metaphysics. For Wittgenstein, the forms of life are the significant mode of meaning *in* language, not a consequence of a significant meaning *for* language.

Despite the daunting task, it is possible to clarify discussions of Wittgenstein on the basis of a distinction between Greek and Hebraic thought. The aspect of Greek thought to be discussed is based on the misplacement of significance from our everyday lives to foundations (e.g. Forms, simple objects) to secure meaning. In other words, thinking takes precedence over looking; the significance of the applications of language – the language-games – is transferred to unseen anchors to secure meaning. On the contrary, Wittgenstein's non-foundational and 'embodied' understanding of language sees our daily activities as significant for meaning, and, on a similar basis, will be shown to be analogical to Hebraic thought in the fourth chapter.

An aspect of 'Greek' thought

The aspect of Greek thought drawn out from Wittgenstein's remark to Drury and used in the following discussion, is the removal of significance from our everyday activities (the corporeal) on the ground that they are inconsequential towards the goal of re-establishment, whereas the re-establishment gives meaning (is consequential) to our everyday lives. Indeed, Rowan Greer says Origen 'does not accord our life in this world a primary reality. But by showing that it points toward an eternal destiny, he gives it a significance it could not otherwise have. Like Plato he wishes to show how our Heraclitean experience is informed and made meaningful by its participation in the Parmenidean world of ultimate reality.'[8] Our world may seem to be changing and fleeting, but the endpoint of a unified re-establishment is thought to impart meaning into our lives. Indeed, it is thought that an unchanging and uniform ground or essence is a necessary requirement for meaning. Thus, any meaning we have in our fleeting and composite worldly lives is subsequent to that of the unified re-establishment.

If our activities are not consequential for the re-establishment, then our bodies can be regarded as less significant than our mind/soul – the former cannot lead to the re-establishment, but at least the latter can grasp the idea of it. For example, in *De Principiis* Origen notes that body and world are obviously active in physical qualities, 'but [the] mind, for its movements or operations, needs no physical space, nor sensible magnitude, nor bodily shape, nor colour, nor any other of those adjuncts which are the properties of body or matter'.[9] For Origen, the body is 'composite and differing' like the world, but the mind is not.[10] Thus, the mind is able to perceive the unity and meaning beyond the world and body, and then subsequently brings meaning back to our lives.[11] Basically, meaning is sought outside our everyday activities. The focus of Origen's theory (the re-establishment) shifts our perspective from our varied human activities and conventions to external realms where finality resides and towards which our worldly activities are inconsequential. In effect, Wittgenstein's remark – 'don't think, but look!'[12] – is inverted to 'don't look, but think!' When we 'look' we see the fleeting and complex Heraclitean world, but by 'thinking' it is thought that we can discern the unchanging foundation behind the world. Once again, the problem with this aspect of thought is *not* that it simply regards everyday activities as superfluous (it would be absurd to regard our everyday activities as completely futile), but that our everyday activities do not reveal the teleological goal of a common and foundational meaning or purpose.

Origen's idea that there is 'something' more significant and unified than our vacillating bodily activities in the world can be seen as similar to Platonic thought. In the *Phaedo* (78D–80C), the soul is understood as unchanging and, by means of pure thought, there is a certainty perceived in the eternal Forms, while a too corporeal and concrete perspective cannot fathom this wisdom. The goal is thereby to free thinking from the confines of the body:

> Then he will do this most perfectly who approaches the object with thought alone, without associating any sight with his thought, or dragging in any sense perception with his reasoning, but who, using pure thought alone, tries to track down reality pure and by itself, freeing himself as far as possible from the eyes and ears, and in a word from the whole body, because the body confuses the soul and does not allow it to acquire truth and wisdom whenever it associates with it.[13]

In contrast to the body that 'confuses the soul' by 'associating sight with thought' (i.e. looking), the philosopher is to strive towards 'pure thought' by 'freeing' oneself from the body. However, since we are bound to a corporeal body, we can at best strive for wisdom by not relying exclusively on our perceptions, which show us only shadows of reality. It should not be surprising then, that in the *Phaedo* the true philosopher is preparing for death where, unlike existence on the earth, wisdom is more easily found:

> It really has been shown to us that, if we are ever to have pure knowledge, we must escape from the body and observe things in themselves with the soul by itself. It seems likely that we shall, only then, when we are dead, attain that which we desire and of which we claim to be lovers, namely, wisdom …[14]

With such an understanding, the soul/reason takes on primary importance in contrast to the complex and fleeting corporeal world and body. Once again, 'thinking' takes precedence over 'looking'.

What we see in the world, in Platonic thought, are only shadows or imitations, but there are exterior Forms of secure meaning. It is thought that there are unambiguous examples, or paradigms, that ground meaning, and although they are not part of the fleeting world, they inform meaning in the world. Only through participation in the ideal Forms is meaning found in the world. The foundational aspect of this theory is based on the idea that Beauty, Triangles, etc. exist as perfect examples upon which our experience of imperfect beauty, triangles, etc. in the world depends. For example, in the *Phaedo* we read that 'if there is anything beautiful besides the Beautiful itself, it is beautiful for no other reason than that it shares in that Beautiful, and I say so with everything'.[15] Thus, the 'soul investigates by itself ... into the realm of what is pure, ever existing, immortal and unchanging',[16] by which 'other things acquired their name by having a share in them'.[17] It is thought that there is a 'realm' beyond our world that provides meaning to our world and enables our ability to have knowledge in the world. In a sense, our world is parasitic on foundational meaning since what is in the world does not give to the eternal Forms but only takes from them.

It is interesting to note that the aspect of Greek thought which seeks anchors outside our lives – and likewise outside our application of language – to secure meaning can also be found in Wittgenstein's early work. In the *Tractatus*, as discussed in the first chapter, Wittgenstein regards our ordinary language as a disguise. He says, 'language disguises thought; so that from the external form of the clothes one cannot infer the form of thought they clothe, because the external form of the clothes is constructed with quite another object than to let the body be recognized'.[18] Wittgenstein wants to uncover the form of thought behind ordinary language, and this postulation of something behind our everyday language can be seen as similar to the Platonic ideal intelligibility behind our fleeting world. It is thought that we need to see through the costume of the world to the basic elements of the world. Dilman notes this similarity between Wittgenstein's Tractarian understanding of language and Greek thought, whereby 'there is an element of realism – linguistic realism – in the *Tractatus* which may be characterized as "Platonic". For it measures natural languages against language with a capital L which exists independently of these languages and the surroundings of human life in which they are used.'[19] In the search for this one form behind our everyday language, the early Wittgenstein attempts to reduce language to its basic parts, down to the simple object that connects to the uniform structure of language. Or in other words, the structure of the world determines the structure of language. Wittgenstein says, 'the picture according to which reality is thought of here is that beauty, death, etc., are the pure (concentrated) substances, whereas in a beautiful object they are contained as an admixture. –And don't I recognize here my own observations about "object" and "complex"?' (Plato).[20] Both Plato and the early Wittgenstein think there is a universal intelligibility behind our fleeting and complex world. Rhees sees this similarity in the following:

> Plato seemed to have thought, as Wittgenstein himself did at one time, that there is some fundamental form which must appear in all discourse in so far as it is intelligible or is to be discourse at all, [but] this view, that understanding or intelligibility is always one thing, is a mistake ... any question about an ideal of intelligibility, or any notion of perfect intelligibility, is probably confused. At least it has not the clear sense which Plato seemed to think it had.[21]

The similarity between the early Wittgenstein and Greek thought resides in the connection for language to a universal template as the foundation for language, while the significance of the diverse human applications of language and contextual understandings – the forms of life – are neglected.[22]

The aspect of Greek thought discussed, be it of classical or contemporary influence, seeks foundations outside of our practice and use of language, and therefore contrasts to Wittgenstein's continued thought. He rejects the idea that our world and the activities in it are not significant for meaning, and the associated idea of foundations that, in contrast to our lives, are significant. Dilman notes the change in Wittgenstein's thought in the following:

> Thus while in the *Tractatus* logic does not need and does not have any metaphysical foundations in an independent reality – 'logic must look after itself' – it is itself a metaphysical foundation of natural languages. Actual languages must conform to it; they are the tail which logic with a capital L, as a top dog, wags. In the *Investigations* this relation is

reversed and the capital L is dropped from both logic and language. We have 'language-games' which involved bodily behaviour; they are organically related in natural languages which are themselves part of human life. They form an important part of the life and culture in which speakers of a language participate. Logic appears in that. It does not have an independent anchor outside or separate from natural languages and the language-games which form part of such languages.[23]

Instead of seeking connections for language outside of our everyday life (i.e. simple objects, pre-established conditions, ideal Forms, etc.), language must connect to the language-games – our activities in the world. Plato maintains a capital '*B*' to define beauty, while, as noted by Dilman, Wittgenstein lets the anchor go and simply describes language and beauty – with no requirement of *L*anguage or *B*eauty.

This distinction between meaning being found in our ordinary activities, in contrast to meaning residing outside our everyday activities, can be seen in Wittgenstein's comment, 'Socrates pulls up the pupil who when asked what knowledge is enumerates cases of knowledge. And Socrates doesn't regard that as even a preliminary step to answering the question. But our answer consists in giving such an enumeration and a few analogies. (In a certain sense we are always making things easier and easier for ourselves in philosophy.)'[24] Wittgenstein regards our description of everyday activities to be the knowledge we have, while Socrates' remark shows an interest in the unity behind language. Thus, Wittgenstein says, 'I cannot characterize my standpoint better than by saying that it is opposed to that which Socrates represents in the Platonic dialogues.'[25] Wittgenstein looks to our ordinary applications of language as primary in discussions of language and meaning, in contrast to the Greek aspect of thought which requires foundational anchors outside our ordinary applications of language to secure meaning.[26] The aspect of Greek thought discussed makes external connections for meaning (e.g. the eternal Forms), and Wittgenstein's Tractarian work makes connections for language (i.e. the simple objects), but for the later Wittgenstein our use of language (i.e. the language-games) is sufficient. Meaning is revealed in the forms of life, it is not hidden behind or above our use of language.

Wittgenstein and the problem of 'disembodied' language

The aspect of Greek thought discussed uses anchors to secure meaning; that is, the anchor hooks onto the foundation of meaning (ideal Forms, pre-established conditions, underlying logical structure, etc.). For example, as previously discussed, the early Wittgenstein thought that the sense of a proposition rests in the relation between the structure of the world (the simple objects) and names – the projective relation to reality. In this sense, the anchor hooks to a simple object embedded in the structure of the world, and then the line is tied to a name. The connection of an object to a name and ultimately to the simple object, in contrast to seeing how the object is applied, is taken as the significant function of meaning in language. In other words, the logical structure of language is primary, while the application of language is secondary. Wittgenstein notes this difficulty:

> In reflecting on language and meaning we can easily get into a position where we think that in philosophy we are not talking of words and sentences in a quite common-or-garden sense, but in a subliminated and abstract sense. – As if a particular proposition wasn't really the thing that some person utters, but an ideal entity (the 'class of all synonymous sentences' or the like). But is the chess knight that the rules of chess deal with such an ideal and abstract entity too? (We are not justified in having any more scruples about our language than the chess player had about chess, namely none.)[27]

By focusing on foundations, we can lose sight of the applications of objects in the world where the significance of meaning resides; that is, by simply giving a chess piece the name knight, we are not much further ahead in understanding what the meaning of 'knight' is. For example, if I am shown an object, such as a book, and I am told that it has the name 'book', it may be thought that I then know what 'book' means. However, I might think 'book' means flat, composed of paper, hard, etc. It is only through using a book (i.e. reading it) that I can know what the term 'book' means. Rhees sees this problem and remarks that it would be 'nonsense to say that it is the meanings of terms that determine how we use them'.[28] We do not attach an external meaning to the object, nor does the object hold an innate meaning that attaches to an underlying logical syntax; rather, through using the object we come to see the meaning of the object (e.g. by reading a book we know the meaning of 'book'). To think that attaching a name to an object is sufficient to grasp meaning in language is overly simplistic.

Nevertheless, Augustine, according to Wittgenstein, falls into this tradition and regards learning language to be a function of the mind independently, as a passive observer of the world, labelling objects in the world – where naming is the quintessence of language. For example, Augustine writes:

> When they (my elders) named some object, and accordingly moved towards something, I saw this and I grasped that the thing was called by the sound they uttered when they meant to point it out. Their intention was shown by their bodily movements, as it were the natural language of all peoples: the expression of the face, the play of the eyes, the movement of the other parts of the body, and the tone of voice which expresses our state of mind in seeking, having, rejecting, or avoiding something. Thus, as I heard words repeatedly used in their proper places in various sentences, I gradually learnt to understand what objects they signified; and after I had trained my mouth to form these signs, I used them to express my own desires.[29]

Wittgenstein discusses Augustine's understanding of language as follows:

> The individual words in language name objects – sentences are combinations of such names. – In this picture of language we find the roots of the following idea: Every word has a meaning. This meaning is correlated with the word. It is the object for which the word stands.[30]

It is thought that Augustine regards words as having a simple and direct meaning that is analogous to definitions in a dictionary. For example, we may read in the dictionary that a knight is a chess piece with the form of a horse's head, but we still would have no idea of how the piece is used in the game of chess. Wittgenstein further says, '[Augustine] talks about how we attach names to things, or understand the names of things. *Naming* here appears as the foundation, the be all and end all of language.'[31] With such definitions, the foundation of language rests on the agent's connection of the name and object – that we can point to the chess piece and say it is a knight – while the application of words and the nexus within which they are used become less significant as a mode of meaning.

Wittgenstein consequently regards Augustine's example of learning a language to be too simple (but not unworkable in *all* cases).[32] Wittgenstein demonstrates that not only is ostensive definition inadequate when referring to objects – such as a knight, in which case we might have thought 'knight' only meant a likeness of a horse's head – but some words also cannot be understood as names in the first place (i.e. they cannot be named objects) such as the exclamations 'Ow!' or 'Fine!'[33] These are expressions in our language that cannot be categorized by an ostensive definition, and that make the difficulty of ostensive definitions more clear. Meaning cannot be found in the name-object relation of the word 'Ow!'; rather, the meaning resides in the application of the word 'Ow!' This example shows that there are words that do not name anything, but that do have established applications. It points to the requirement of looking at the application of words and, to use an analogy, not simply setting our anchor on a distant foundation that it can never reach – but this is not because the sea is, so to speak, too deep; rather, there is no ground outside applications.

Augustine's theory, according to Wittgenstein, not only simplifies language into names and objects, which erroneously assumes the purpose of language is simply the name-object relation, but also implies that the subject has an innate language prior to learning by means of ostensive definition.[34] Wittgenstein notes that Augustine's ostensive definition 'describes the learning of human language as if the child came into a strange country; and did not understand the language of the country; that is, as if it already had a language, only not this one'.[35] For example, when learning a second language I can understanding the meaning of '*livre*' simply by attaching the name '*livre*' to the object which I understand in my native language to be a book. One way for ostensive definition to work is to already know a language and to take the background of the known language to the unknown language. In other words, my under-standing of an ostensive definition for '*livre*' depends on my understanding of the applications of the term 'book'.

Wittgenstein notes that when we try to explain how we know something, such as the word 'book', we often forget the applications and 'keep on steering towards the idea of the private ostensive definition'. However, he continues, we 'could not apply any rules to a *private* transition from what is seen to words. Here the rules really would hang in the air; for the institution of their use is lacking.'[36] Once again, we would be trying to set our anchor, but there is no ground for the anchor to grip without taking account of the practices associated with words. Rhees also sees the difficulties with separating thought and language from the world and states:

> In language it makes a difference what you say. But how can it make any difference what you say privately? (I do not mean talking to yourself.) It seems that in a private language everything would have to be at once a statement and a definition.[37]

In other words, we can only understand words by referring to something, and they cannot refer to anything unless the language is spoken. Hence, if a language was abstracted from society it would make no difference what is said, so nothing is understood. When language is understood as based on naming instead of application, that is, when it is cut out from the world, then we easily fall into the idea that our mind discerns the link between an object and its name without need of the community of language we inherit. But it is the surroundings – the concrete and the whole – not the private retreat that affords meaning.

Thus, in contrast to turning to private ostensive definitions, Wittgenstein remarks: 'How do I know this colour is red? – It would be an answer to say: I have learnt English.'[38] There is no need for introspection or metaphysical connections; all we need to understand the meaning of words is the use of our language. In contrast to meaning being a matter of underlying logical structures or mental deliberations, the 'meaning of a word is a kind of employment of it. For it is what we learn when the word is incorporated into our language.'[39] For example, 'Children do not learn that books exist, that armchairs exist, etc., etc., – they learn to fetch books, sit in armchairs, etc., etc.'[40] They do not need to learn any super logic behind the use of words. Furthermore, 'it is part of the grammar of the word "chair" that *this* is what we call "to sit in a chair" ';[41] the children do not initiate serious introspection in order to understand what is actually used in their lives. What is significant, and must be taken seriously, are the language and bodies we have, rather than Tractarian simple objects, a universal foundation, or an inner spirit or mind behind the trappings of language and the body. Hence, Wittgenstein says, 'to imagine a language is to imagine a form of life'.[42]

When we look at our language – our form of life – we see the dynamic and shifting applications of language in contrast to perceiving a unified intelligibility sought in Greek thought. Wittgenstein writes: 'Our language can be seen as an ancient city: a maze of little streets and squares, of old and new houses, and of houses with additions from various periods; and this surrounded by a multitude of new boroughs with straight regular streets and uniform houses.'[43] He sees the ancient city as our language based on deeds that lead through crooked streets, not on an ideal blueprint that is more or less imitated. The suburbs are a refinement, but they are not the better representation of the essence of language, for how could we even imagine this essence or any progress in regards to it? Wittgenstein writes: 'How strange if logic were concerned with an "ideal" language and not with *ours*. For what would this ideal language express?'[44] Nevertheless, while the Greek aspect of thought discussed wants to approximate the ideal blueprint which informs language and assumes that it thereby gets ever closer to the foundational meaning, Wittgenstein notes:

> We have got on to slippery ice where there is no friction and so in a certain sense the conditions are ideal, but also, just because of that, we are unable to walk. We want to walk: so we need *friction*. Back to the rough ground![45]

Any attempt to grasp the foundations of language (as if it were possible) in search of the ideal strips us of the language we have and sends us back slipping on the ice or hanging our anchors in thin air.

With an understanding of embodiment, however, we stay on rough ground with Wittgenstein's thought. Rather than regarding the mind as the means of perceiving the intelligibility of the foundation for language, Wittgenstein points to the simple use of language in the world. In a sense, there is a certain humbleness that results in Wittgenstein's thought; namely, since language is associated with the irregular streets, and thought is coextensive with language,[46] it then follows that the mind is fixed to these very streets – not a 'pure' ideal. Any attempt to transcend the labyrinth of language to find an ideal straight street is an immodest pursuit that can only find chimeras. Thus, Wittgenstein writes,

> I might say: if the place I want to get to could only be reached by way of a ladder, I would give up trying to get there. For the place I really have to get to is a place I must already be at now. Anything that I might reach by climbing a ladder does not interest me.[47]

Our actions and reactions – our use of language – must be seen as the mode of meaning, not a consequence of meaning. We need to throw away the ladder given to us through the Greek aspect of thought discussed (and the *Tractatus*) and instead learn on the ground. We can then look for a better religious analogy for Wittgenstein's religious point of view along our meandering streets rather than in distant and foreign ideals.

Back to the ground: 'embodied' language and religion

In discussions of religion we may erroneously assume that dualism is a natural epistemological stance; perhaps the body is thought to be inferior to the soul, but religion can be read along with Wittgenstein's thought as *looking* at our 'earthly life' as a significant mode of meaning, in contrast to *thinking* of absolutes and ideals. Rhees notes:

> When Plato speaks of the form of good in the *Republic*, he does not say that the sensible world, and earthly life, is any sort of imitation or likeness of that. He insists that there cannot be any representation or appearance of the good ... And I do not think that Plato's conception of aspiration towards an ideal can be much like the Christian conception of God.[48]

We need to see that there are aspects of understanding in religion that are more closely related to Wittgenstein's thought than Greek thought. Just as children learn the word 'chair' through the use of a chair, as noted above, so Rhees writes:

> Children learn a theology when they learn how the word 'God' is used ... the question of 'what God is' could only be answered through

'coming to know God' in worship and in religious life. 'To know God is to worship him'.[49]

Rather than explaining 'chair', for example, through the concepts of gravity, geometry, density, etc., we turn to the use of a chair in our lives. Likewise, knowing God is a part of life and worship, and can only be understood through religious applications. Winch similarly writes, 'religious uses of language equally, I want to say, are not descriptions of an "order of reality" distinct from the earthly life with which we are familiar. These uses of language do, however, have an application in what religious people say and do in the course of their life on earth; and this is where their "relationship to reality" is to be sought.'[50] In order to understand religion, it is necessary to look at the examples and practices of religion in the world, in contrast to disembodying religion by focusing on ideals and concepts external to their form of life.

In the *Tractatus* and the *Investigations* there is the similar goal to understand the nature of language. In the *Tractatus* it is that elusive thing below the surface, but in the *Investigations* it is on the ground and open to view.[51] Isaac Nevo notes this change in the contrast between Wittgenstein's 'non-historical appeal to God as an unrevealed, or "indifferent" deity, in the *Tractatus*, with his expression of religious belief in *Culture and Value*, wherein the traditional framework of revealed religion is accepted'.[52] Just as language is the revealed meaning, that is, meaning is not behind the disguise of language, so we must look at what religion shows us, instead of hypothetical concepts behind religion. This later understanding is found in Wittgenstein's notes:

> Christianity is not a doctrine, not, I mean, a theory about what has happened and will happen to the human soul, but a description of something that actually takes place in human life. For 'consciousness of sin' is a real event and so are despair and salvation through faith. Those who speak of such things ... are simply describing what has happened to them, whatever gloss anyone may want to put on it.[53]

Description takes the place of explanation, and faith takes over from silence. The point is that faith is a means of discourse, that there is a 'transition from mystic, nondiscursive silence towards an unrevealed deity to faith in the revealed deity of the historical narrative'.[54] The earthly practices and history of language take on new significance for meaning in language and religion; as Wittgenstein says, 'God grant the philosopher insight into what lies in front of our eyes.'[55] Note that he does not add, 'And let us think through to the ultimate logic or foundation behind what is in front of our eyes.' What language and religion rest upon is not a solid structure of atoms, or an ideal foundation, but a changing form of life – humanity.[56]

The idealistic desire to disembody language or religion from applications does not fit with Wittgenstein's thought. If we do not pay attention to the surroundings and applications of language and instead climb the ladders of abstraction, then what are we left with? Wittgenstein writes: 'Is it, as it were, a contamination of the sense that we express it in a particular language which has accidental features, and not as it were bodiless and pure?'[57] Furthermore: 'We are talking about spatial and temporal phenomena of language, not about some non-spatial, non-temporal phantasm.'[58]

Wittgenstein rebels against abstract philosophy by looking at the concrete applications of language, instead of attempting to perceive ideal foundations. A good example of the contrast between an idealism that devalues the significance of human life and the concrete person can be found in Dostoevsky's novel *The Brothers Karamazov*. This work was known and appreciated by Wittgenstein who 'read [it] so often he knew whole passages of it by heart'.[59] Moreover, 'one of the few personal possessions Wittgenstein packed [on his way to the Russian front in 1916] was a copy of *The Brothers Karamazov*'.[60]

Dostoevsky brings the important conception of the body and soul as unified into relief through the counter example of Ivan who represents 'thinking' and the neglect of 'looking'.[61] Nicolas Berdyaev insightfully observes:

Philosophy of this kind [Idealism] tends to sacrifice the human soul to the Absolute Spirit. It is a sacrifice of the personality and humanity. It is a philosophy of abstract spirit. And man, living concrete man, must rebel against such an interpretation of spirit.[62]

Ivan is not interested in humanity; he sacrifices the human soul to abstraction by turning to abstract Euclidean ideas.[63] He says, 'one can love one's neighbour in the abstract, and sometimes even at a distance, but at close quarters it is almost impossible'.[64] The closer Ivan approaches the flesh, the coarse, the material, and the humble, the more difficult it becomes for him to find meaning since these factors are much more messy and unsystematic than mathematics.[65] Unsurprisingly, the death of Zosima and his decomposing body is a further obstacle that repulses Ivan to retreat even further from reality (looking) to Euclidean calculus (thinking) to escape the worldly.[66]

Ferapont additionally renounces the body and ties the fetid flesh of Zosima's body to Satan by means of the cherry jam Zosima enjoyed with the ladies of the community: 'He was seduced by sweets ... he sipped tea, he worshipped his belly, filling it with sweet things and his mind with haughty thought ... and for this he is put to shame.'[67] One cannot help but to think of Socrates' response to Simmias in the *Phadeo*, 'Do you think it is the part of a philosopher to be concerned with such so-called pleasures as those of food and drink?' and Simmias's reply, 'I think the true philosopher despises them.'[68] In the interest of the ideal, reason is placed on a pedestal, while the worldly is condemned.

Yet the distance created by Ivan and Ferapont between the Satanic tea and cherry jam, and the ideal is too great to bear. Embodiment is shown by Dostoevsky as a condition of spirituality, not as a deterrent.[69] Zosima is an example of the unity of spirit and body active in the world. The ladies, tea and cherry jam are the means of understanding, not the vices of Satan that obscure the pure, or the deceptions of an evil being. This lesson is learned by Alesha who, in contrast to Ivan, appears to understand Zosima and begins to embrace the material world. The words and actions of Zosima in life, and his body in death, may lead Ivan to distance thought from the body and the world, but Alesha accepts the material world and rejects the trend of disembodiment represented by Ivan. In contrast to the tendency to separate the body and spirit, Dostoevsky views the body itself as a spiritual metaphor.[70]

Wittgenstein similarly states, 'the human body is the best picture of the human soul',[71] and 'the face is the soul of the body'.[72] What we see, then, in another human being is the revealed person, not a veil behind which the true person resides. Berdyaev writes:

The antithesis, spirit or flesh, is an error. The antithesis is only conceivable when *flesh* is regarded as sin rather than as a natural part of the human constitution. The Cartesian dualism of spirit and body is entirely wrong ... man is a whole creature, an organism compounded of spirit, soul and body. The body is an integral part of the human personality, image and likeness.[73]

Language and learning, and the soul and body, are best understood when we look at ordinary life and language, and only become difficult concepts as we begin to separate them. Just as we should not regard language as a disguise behind which logical syntax resides, so we should not view the body as a disguise behind which the 'real' person as mind/soul resides. Even Descartes, despite his assumed dualism and seclusion of his thoughts from the world, does not as strongly separate the mind and body when he simply looks at ordinary life: 'It is the ordinary course of life and conversation, and the abstention from meditation ... that teaches us how to conceive of the union of souls and the body.' [Letter to Elizabeth, 28 June 1643][74] Furthermore, Descartes states, 'the body and soul, in relation to the whole human being, are incomplete substances; and it follows from their being incomplete that what they constitute is an *ens per se* [an essential entity in contrast to an accidental quality]'.[75] For these reasons, Descartes writes, 'I am not merely present in my body as a sailor is present in a ship, but I am very closely joined and, as it were, intermingled with it, so that I and the body form a unit.'[76] He notes that our bodies are not like a sailing vessel since we feel pain as part of ourselves, whereas in the case of the sailing vessel we simply observe the damage. The body and soul belong together, the 'true person' is not the 'inner person', and contemplation and feeling are not superior to the actions of the body which are equally as important and meaningful.[77]

Given the importance that Wittgenstein places upon the 'whole' person, it is not surprising when he comments: 'it is my soul, with its passions, as it were with its flesh and blood, that must be saved, not my abstract mind'.[78] Could anyone think that the 'soul' of a flower resides in the scent alone, while the colour and physical structure of the flower and stem are of secondary importance? Likewise, how can we think meaning resides behind our ordinary language? The flower is a plant with a cellulose and water structure, and it would be senseless to regard the scent as the reality of the flower, but the plant as dispensable. If our plant begins to wither, we water it; we do not simply capture its scent in a bottle and regard that to be sufficient. Instead of some abstract notion of scent or soul, each person is a flesh and blood being who breathes, sleeps, eats, etc.; this is the person to whom Wittgenstein points.[79] Dietrich Bonhoeffer takes this point to the extreme in saying that we can only understand the 'Divine, not in absolutes, but in the natural form of man'.[80] Not only is the human being a whole only with the body, but even the Divine can only be known bodily. We cannot know the absolutes, but we do have a very close understanding of a flesh and blood existence.

We have seen that Greek thought is typified as not taking our (bodily) use of language in the world as a significant mode of meaning, but instead positing foundational realms outside our everyday lives to secure meaning. In contrast to this type of Greek thought, and as noted by Engelmann, Wittgenstein 'was never a mystic in the sense of occupying his mind with mystic-gnostic fantasies. Nothing was further from his mind than the attempt to paint a picture of a world beyond (either before or after death), about which we cannot speak.'[81] Moreover, Monk notes that the 'purpose of [the language-games] is to free ourselves from the philosophical confusions that result from considering language in isolation from its place in the "stream of life"'.[82] If we are to discuss a religious point of view in relation to Wittgenstein, then it must relate to his thought by being equally 'embodied' in the 'stream of life', without attempting to set anchors for meaning in foundational categories, pre-established conditions, instincts, ideal Forms, a universal determined future, underlying logical structures, or, in short, thin air.

To attempt to set an anchor in these abstract categories (which is an aspect of Greek thought) only leads to metaphysical confusion, not clarity. However, when we look at language and religion set in the 'stream of life', then we describe particular practices and clarify the nature of the analogy being made. In particular, Hebraic thought (a particular strand of which will be discussed in the fourth chapter) will be shown to be a specific religious analogy for Wittgenstein's later thought since they both are distinct from the aspect of Greek thought discussed above, they disregard metaphysics, and similarly base meaning and authority in the concrete applications of language (theology) in the form of life.

Endnotes

1   Winch, 'Discussion of Malcolm's Essay', 108.
2   Once again, Drury states: 'Origen taught that at the end of time there would be a final restitution of all things. That even Satan and the fallen angels would be restored to their former glory.' ('Conversations with Wittgenstein', 161) Origen's idea of *apokatastasis* (re-establishment) signifies that, through time, all return to God: 'The end is always like the beginning.' Origen, *De Principiis*, in *Ante-Nicene Fathers*, ed. Alexander Roberts and James Donaldson, vol. 4 (Buffalo: Christian Literature Publishing, 1887), I, vi, 2. The implication is an ultimate return to an incorporeal existence in God, regardless of our worldly activities.
3   Drury, 'Conversations with Wittgenstein', 161.
4   We can also make a comparison here with Calvin's predestination, as discussed previously, in which case what we do now is irrelevant as a means to salvation.
5   *Ibid.*, 161.
6   Wittgenstein, *Philosophical Investigations*, p. 226.
7   *Ibid.*, § 66.
8   Rowan A. Greer, 'Introduction' in *Origen*, trans. and intro. by Rowan A. Greer (Mahwah, NJ: Paulist Press, 1979), 28.
9   Origen, *De Principiis*, I, i, 6.
10 *Ibid.* Similarly, we read in Calvinism, a basis of Shields's theory, that the soul is to be freed of the 'prison-house of the body', 'men cleaving too much to the earth are dull of apprehension', and, unsurprisingly, the soul is the 'nobler part'. Calvin, *Institutes of the Christian Religion*, bk 1, ch. 15, sec. 2.
11 Origen, *De Principiis*, I, i, 7.
12 Wittgenstein, *Philosophical Investigations*, § 66.
13 Plato, *Phaedo*, trans. G. M. A. Grube (Indianapolis: Hackett Publishing, 1977), 66a.
14 *Ibid.*, 66e.

15 *Ibid.*, 100e.

16 *Ibid.*, 79d.

17 *Ibid.*, 102b.

18 Wittgenstein, *Tractatus Logico-Philosophicus*, 4.002.

19 İlham Dilman, 'Wittgenstein and the Question of Linguistic Idealism' (n.p., n.d.), 3.

20 Wittgenstein, 'Sections 86–93 (pp. 405–35) of the so-called "Big Typescript"', 21.

21 Rhees, *Rush Rhees on Religion and Philosophy*, 186.

22 It is very important to note that although Wittgenstein and Greek thought posit foundations for language that are outside our everyday experience, Wittgenstein nevertheless keeps language anchored to the world. He does not regard the simple object, for instance, as an abstract ideal; instead, it is a structural element of the world.

23 Dilman, 'Wittgenstein and the Question of Linguistic Idealism', 3.

24 Wittgenstein, *Philosophical Grammar*, 120–1.

25 Wittgenstein, *The so-called Diktat Für Schlick* (approx. 1931–33), 302: 14.

26 Wittgenstein's emphasis on our everyday lives in the world does not, however, de-emphasize the unsayable; rather, it remains the most significant aspect of his thought, but not as a foundation for language. The unsayable retains the mystery of religion, ethics, value, etc., whose value is *outside* the world, while language is *in* the world. The unsayable does not determine or inform language. Wittgenstein regards the unsayable as beyond the realm of language entirely, and to make any connection between the unsayable and language leads to metaphysics and confusion, not clarity. In contrast, the aspect of Greek thought discussed above takes the transcendent to be the most significant mode and foundation of language and meaning, and thereby devalues our activities in the world as imitations of the transcendent.

27 Wittgenstein, *Philosophical Grammar*, 121.

28 Rush Rhees, *Wittgenstein and the Possibility of Discourse*, ed. D. Z. Phillips (Cambridge: Cambridge University Press, 1998), 87.

29 Augustine, *Confessions*, bk I, ch 8. Wittgenstein, *Philosophical Investigations*, § 1.

30   *Ibid.*, § 1.

31   Wittgenstein, *Philosophical Grammar*, 56.

32   *Ibid.*, 57.

33   Wittgenstein, *Philosophical Investigations*, § 27.

34   We can find the devaluation of the everyday use of language as the mode of meaning in Noam Chomsky and Jerry Fodor, both of whom posit a foundation for language. We find the idea of an innate inner reason, or ability, that enables language in Chomsky's work. He writes: 'As a precondition for language learning, he must possess, first, a linguistic theory that specifies the form of the grammar of a possible human language, and, second, a strategy for selecting a grammar of the appropriate form that is compatible with the primary linguistic data.' *Aspects of the Theory of Syntax* (Cambridge, MS: MIT Press, 1965), 25. The logical conclusion of Chomsky's theory is noted, and endorsed, by Fodor, namely, 'one cannot learn that P falls under R unless one has a language in which P and R can be represented. So one cannot learn a language unless one has a language'. *The Language of Thought* (Hassocks, Sussex: Harvester Press, 1975), 64.

35   Wittgenstein, *Philosophical Investigations*, § 32.

36   *Ibid.*, § 380.

37   Rush Rhees, 'Can There be a Private Language', in *Discussions of Wittgenstein*, 61.

38   Wittgenstein, *Philosophical Investigations*, § 381.

39   Wittgenstein, *On Certainty*, 61.

40   *Ibid.*, 476.

41   Ludwig Wittgenstein, *The Blue and Brown Books* (Oxford: Basil Blackwell, 1972), 24.

42   Wittgenstein, *Philosophical Investigations*, § 19.

43   *Ibid.*, § 18.

44   Ludwig Wittgenstein, *Philosophical Remarks*, ed. Rush Rhees, trans. Raymond Hargreaves and Roger White (Oxford: Basil Blackwell, 1975), 52.

45   Wittgenstein, *Philosophical Investigations*, § 107. Nietzsche makes an interesting comparison on this point: 'Where man cannot find anything to see or grasp, he has no further business – that is certainly an imperative different from the Platonic one ... we have nothing

but *rough* work to do.' Friedrich Nietzsche, *Beyond Good and Evil*, trans. Helen Zimmern and Walter Kaufmann (New York: Vintage Books, 1966), part I, 22.

46   Wittgenstein, *Philosophical Investigations*, § 329.

47   Wittgenstein, *Culture and Value*, 7e.

48   Rhees, *Rush Rhees on Religion and Philosophy*, 181.

49   *Ibid.*, 44.

50   Winch, *Trying to Make Sense*, 26.

51   Wittgenstein, *Philosophical Investigations*, § 92.

52   Isaac Nevo, 'Religious Belief and Jewish Identity in Wittgenstein's Philosophy', *Philosophy Research Archives*, 13 (1987–88), 226.

53   Wittgenstein, *Culture and Value*, 28e.

54   Nevo, 'Religious Belief and Jewish Identity', 234.

55   Wittgenstein, *Culture and Value*, 63e.

56   The idea that this then leads to relativism and indeterminacy is countered in Chapter 4.

57   Wittgenstein, *Philosophical Grammar*, 108.

58   *Ibid.*, 121.

59   Monk, *The Duty of Genius*, 136.

60   *Ibid.*

61   Denis Patrick Slattery, 'Corrupting Corpse vs. Reasoned Abstraction: The Play of Evil in *The Brothers Karamazov*', *Dostoevsky Studies*, 1, no. 1 (1993), 9.

62   Nicolas Berdyaev, *Spirit and Reality*, trans. George Reavey (London: Geoffrey Bles: The Centenary Press, 1939), 41. Friedrich Nietzsche also rebels against idealism, 'I should prefer to describe the entire phenomenon "Plato" by the harsh term "higher swindle" or, if you prefer, "idealism", than by any other.' *Twilight of The Idols*, trans. R. J. Hollingdale (Harmondsworth: Penguin, 1968), 106.

63   Fyodor Dostoevsky, *The Brothers Karamazov* (New York: W. W. Norton, 1976), 179. An interesting analogy can be found at this point; namely, just as Wittgenstein reduced his logic in the *Tractatus* to simple objects, which he could never find, so in Ivan is someone who looks into calculus and then misses the flesh.

64   Dostoevsky, *The Brothers Karamazov*, 184.

65   Wittgenstein's quotation of Grillpazer suits this very situation: 'It's easy to wander about amongst great objects in the distant regions,

so hard to grasp the solitary thing that's right in front of you.' *Culture and Value*, 13e.

66 Nietzsche notes a characteristic of Plato's that can be seen to be similar to Ivan's: '*Courage* in the face of reality ultimately distinguishes such natures as Thucydides and Plato: Plato is a coward in the face of reality – consequently he flees into the ideal.' *Twilight of The Idols*, 107.

67 Dostoevsky, *The Brothers Karamazov*, 312–14.

68 Plato, *Phaedo*, 64d–e.

69 Slattery, 'Corrupting Corpse vs. Reasoned Abstraction', 14.

70 *Ibid.*, 4.

71 Wittgenstein, *Philosophical Investigations*, p. 178.

72 Wittgenstein, *Culture and Value*, 23e.

73 Berdyaev, *Spirit and Reality*, 40.

74 *The Philosophical Writings of Descartes*, 3:227.

75 *Ibid.*, 3:200.

76 *The Philosophical Writings of Descartes*, 2:56.

77 Alvyn Pettersen, *Athanasius and the Human Body* (Bristol: Bristol Press, 1990), 21.

78 Wittgenstein, *Culture and Value*, 33e. Wittgenstein also notes that 'it is humiliating to have to appear like an empty tube which is inflated by a mind'. (11e)

79 D. H. Lawrence makes an interesting comment on the importance of humanity: 'My great religion is a belief in the blood, the flesh, as being wiser than the intellect. We can go wrong in our minds. But what our blood feels and believes and says, is always true. The intellect is only a bit and bridle. What do I care about knowledge. All I want is to answer to my blood, direct, without fribbling intervention of mind, moral, or what not. I conceive a man's body as a kind of flame, like a candle flame forever upright yet flowing: and the intellect is just the light that is shed onto the things around … We have got so ridiculously mindful, that we never know that we ourselves are anything – we think there are only objects we shine on … That is why I like to live in Italy. The people are so unconscious. They only feel and want: they don't know. We know too much. No, we only *think* we know such a lot.' *The Letters of D. H. Lawrence*, ed. J. T. Boulton, vol. 1 (Cambridge: Cambridge University Press, 1979), 503.

80   Dietrich Bonhoeffer, *Letters and Papers from Prison* (London: SCM Press, 1971), 376.

81   Engelmann, *Letters from Wittgenstein*, 79.

82   Monk, *The Duty of Genius*, 330.

4

Wittgenstein's Later Philosophy and Hebraic Thought

The former discussion has shown that it is Wittgenstein's later understanding of language and conception of philosophy that are best suited
to a discussion of an analogical religious point of view. The aim is not to
discern in any absolute sense what Wittgenstein's 'religious point of view'
is, but what religious point of view can be said to be analogical to his later
philosophy. Discussing a specific religious point of view is helpful to more
clearly show the distinct character of Wittgenstein's later philosophy, and
the nature of the analogical relation. Starting with Winch's point, we
can look for a form of religious belief towards which Wittgenstein may
be inclined:

> The position is not hopeless. We are not in the business of trying to
> arrive at a definition, or even a characterization, of religious belief that
> would cover all cases. We need only consider the forms of religious
> belief toward which Wittgenstein himself was most sympathetic or felt
> himself most inclined.[1]

However, unlike Winch, who considers it difficult if not impossible to find
a specific religious analogy, there is an analogy that fits with Wittgenstein's
thought, both naturally and by his own admission. A simple place to
start looking for the religion towards which Wittgenstein was inclined is
found in Hebraic thought. Once again, Wittgenstein remarks to Drury
in conversation:

> Of course it [Origen's idea[2]] was rejected. It would make nonsense of
> everything else. If what we do now is to make no difference in the end,
> then all the seriousness of life is done away with. Your religious ideas
> have always seemed to me more Greek than biblical. Whereas my
> thoughts are one hundred percent Hebraic.[3]

As shown in the previous chapter, this quote distances Greek thought from Wittgenstein's thought. Conversely, Wittgenstein's direct reference to Hebraic thought – that his thought is 'one hundred percent Hebraic' – naturally leads to a discussion of how Hebraic is the type of thought towards which Wittgenstein is inclined.[4] While previous studies have cast Wittgenstein in a Greek light, and have often assumed that Wittgenstein views his Jewish background and Jewish thought in general negatively, this discussion will show that, on the contrary, Hebraic thought is a genuinely fruitful analogy for his later philosophy, and that he does not view his Jewish background or Jewish thought negatively.

It is important to note, however, that just as no attempt has been made in the former chapter to demarcate Greek thought, neither will such an attempt be made with Hebraic thought. Moreover, it is obvious that it is impossible to reduce Greek or Hebraic thought to one definition. Hence, this discussion does not intend or pretend to be discussing 'normative Judaism'. Nor is it the intent of this discussion to cover the history of Jewish thought. Rather, one aspect of Hebraic thought is selected on the basis of its similarity with Wittgenstein's later philosophy. This discussion focuses on a strand of Jewish thought that originates in the classical rabbinic Judaism of Judea and continues, for example, through Rabbi Akiba and Solomon Schechter.[5]

Schechter, as one representative of the strand of Hebraic thought selected, is closer to the 'Talmudists of the age of Hillel and Rabbi Akiba, than to that of Rabbi Saadia Gaon and Maimonides. These later scholars had lived in the midst of ... philosophy of the Middle Ages and were inevitably exposed to alien theological, ethical, and religious ideas'.[6] Schechter had little interest in Maimonides or his philosophical predecessors and followers.[7] He perceived them to be forcing extraneous principles (such as Aristotelian logic) onto rabbinic Judaism, and consequently to be transforming a 'living' Judaism into a 'series of ponderous volumes and unappreciated dogmas'.[8] The strand of Hebraic thought in line with Schechter emphasizes the diversity of Jewish theology in contrast to the more systematic thought of medieval Jewish philosophy. He will be shown to view Judaism not as a '"system" of belief but, rather, of conduct.... (which can never become a logical system, for it arises from a variety of human needs)'.[9] A significant differentiation within Jewish thought exists between classical rabbinic thought and medieval Jewish philosophy. Attempts, such as Maimonides, to harmonize Jewish thought with Greek philosophy diverge from classical rabbinic thought; indeed, Max Kadushin says, 'Medieval Jewish philosophy is not a development or continuation of rabbinic thought.'[10]

The similarity between the particular strand of Hebraic thought selected and Wittgenstein's later philosophy will be shown to reside in their associated focus on human practices and the form of life, in contrast to a formal unity. A similar distinction was noted in the previous chapter, where it was observed that Wittgenstein's later philosophy contrasts with an aspect of formal unity found in Greek thought. Moreover, Rhees regards the Hebrew view of life to be distinct from that of the Greek, as represented by Plato.[11] He sees the distinction residing in the Greek tendency to place a great significance on the 'Parmenidean unity of being, or unity of discourse', in contrast to the Hebrew focus on human life.[12] Dodd also notes this distinction in the following:

> For the Greek, to know God means to contemplate the ultimate reality ... in its changeless essence. For the Hebrew, to know God is to acknowledge Him in His works and to respond to His claims. While for the Greek knowledge of God is the most highly abstract form of pure contemplation, for the Hebrew it is essentially intercourse with God; it is to experience His dealings with men in time, and to hear and obey His commands.[13]

In other words, Greek thought, as shown in the previous chapter, is concerned with foundational meaning beyond everyday experiences (i.e. thinking), but Hebraic thought will be shown to find meaning in their practices and history (i.e. looking). The Hebrew lives by the principle that 'one's relation to God *is* the worship of God'.[14] The practice of worship shows the Hebrews' understanding of their God; thus, 'a religious man on his knees requires no commentator'.[15] For the Greek, by contrast, the intellect seeks the ideal conceptual realms (e.g. the Forms) outside the corporeal world and the philosopher (in both Plato's and Shields's conceptions) is the one who must explain and commentate.

The distinction between Hebraic thought (understood in the line of classical rabbinic Judaism) and Wittgenstein's on the one hand, and Greek thought and Shields's on the other, can be shown through the example of the Israelites and the golden calf. The golden calf provides an example of how confusion within a religious context is analogical to confusion within Wittgenstein's later conception of language. In both cases, religious and philosophical, confusion will be shown to be the result of detaching meaning and authority from the form of life, and wrongly placing them in idols (e.g. golden calf, intermediaries). The treatment for confusion, then, is to destroy the idols that are detached from the form of life and return to the concrete applications of language (theology) and practices within the form of life.

Shields, however, views the confusion of the golden calf in terms that are more closely related to a Tractarian position. He will be shown, in contrast to Wittgenstein's later philosophy and Hebraic thought, to view confusion as a detachment from the 'ground of meaning'. Consequently, Shields attempts to *resolve* the problems of the golden calf and philosophical confusion by offering the 'correct' conceptual structure (i.e. pre-established conditions and 'ground of meaning'), while Hebraic thought and Wittgenstein will be shown to *dissolve* these problems by turning away from conceptual theories to practices that constitute the form of life.

It is important to note that I am not attempting to prove that Wittgenstein's thought is actually Hebraic. Instead, Wittgenstein's later philosophy will be compared to a particular strand of Hebraic thought to show an interesting analogy (e.g. they eschew absolute systems and theories in favour of concrete viewpoints) that illuminates the distinct nature of Wittgenstein's thought.

Hebraic links to Wittgenstein

When one initially thinks of Judaism and Wittgenstein, one recalls such remarks as: 'The Jew is a desert region'[16] and 'The Jewish mind does not have the power to produce even the tiniest flower or blade of grass.'[17] It is sometimes assumed, then, that the only relation between Wittgenstein and Judaism is simply a negative one, with Wittgenstein regarding the latter as inept. Once Wittgenstein is judged in this light, it is easy to think that he must be anti-Semitic. Unfortunately, this disparaging understanding of Wittgenstein and Judaism is not uncommon. Nevo, for instance, considers Wittgenstein's remarks to be 'self-directed anti-Semitism',[18] and states that his 'acceptance of the racial, anti-Semitic stereotype is a striking feature of *C & V*'.[19]

Rhees also relates an incident where Wittgenstein mentions to Mrs Pascal in 1937 that he failed to make clear his Jewish ancestry,[20] thus being regarded as seeing his own Jewish heritage in a negative light. Rhees notes, however, that Wittgenstein 'was never worried about his Jewish ancestry, and I have never heard of anyone who said Wittgenstein tried to conceal it from him. Mrs Pascal writes, as we should expect, that she is "absolutely sure that Wittgenstein never made a false statement about his racial origins".'[21] It is a mistake, according to Rhees, to place Wittgenstein in the same position as Weininger, who did view his own Jewish character negatively, and Rhees says that we should distinguish between the two:

> Weininger writes as though, if I recognise what is Jewish in my thought and feeling, I have a sense of guilt, of something I would overcome if I could. In Wittgenstein there is nothing of this. I may feel guilt for failing to recognise my Jewish traits, for trying to measure them as I measure non-Jewish traits or writings, as though there were no difference. But the Jewish character I finally see, and ought to have seen all along, is no more something I deplore than a non-Jewish trait is.[22]

Indeed, Rhees says, 'Weininger said that for a Jew the "solution" would be an "*overcoming*" of what was Jewish in himself. And Wittgenstein said nothing of the kind.'[23] Evidence is lacking to prove the claim that Wittgenstein views his Jewish background negatively.

Nevertheless, Yuval Lurie takes the Pascal incident to be an 'effort by Wittgenstein to renounce views and attitudes about Jews ingrained in him by his cultural background; views and attitudes from which he now desired to dissociate himself'.[24] Lurie continues this unfortunate line of thought and considers Wittgenstein's remarks on Jewish traits to be 'horrifying':

> For those of us who have grown accustomed to the *Philosophical Investigations*, these remarks are also a source of great astonishment. (Perhaps such as one feels at suddenly discovering a skeleton in the

closet of a close acquaintance.) For behind all the talk about 'spirit' and 'culture' there seem to reverberate familiar anti-Semitic strains.[25]

Gerhard D. Wassermann, who considers Wittgenstein to be a 'Jewish self-denigrator', regards Lurie to be correct, and to have given an 'excellent *exposition* of Wittgenstein's defamatory generalizations about Jews'.[26] He thinks, however, that Wittgenstein's negative Jewish generalizations can be refuted.[27] In doing so, Wassermann gives an extensive list of gifted Jewish thinkers, musicians, poets, artists, scientists, etc. and concludes:

> I have now demonstrated, by citing numerous counter-examples and by noting the formally wrong structure of Wittgenstein's empirical generalizations about Jews, that these generalizations are *totally* wrong ... it was people who argued like him [Wittgenstein] about Jews, that helped to lay the foundations of the Holocaust, in which some of my friends and family perished.[28]

Such a demonstration to prove that there are actually ingenious Jewish individuals is not necessary, nor does it refute Wittgenstein's point, in fact, both Lurie and Wassermann miss Wittgenstein's point. Instead of playing upon the theme of Wittgenstein's supposed critical and anti-Semitic inclinations, we need to re-examine the derisive discussion and, after doing so, we will see that Wittgenstein actually holds Jewish thought in high regard. The possibility of greatness in Jewish thought is not an issue – it is a given. Indeed, it will be shown that Wittgenstein views Jewish thought as exemplary not because it is creative – many styles of thought are creative – but because, like Wittgenstein's thought, it is uniquely based on the concrete. In this case, there is no need to 'prove' in opposition to Wittgenstein's writings that the Jewish mind can be brilliant, for if we look carefully at Wittgenstein's work we can see that he does so himself! Furthermore, the whole conception of needing to prove that there are Jewish intellectuals is blatantly absurd, as if we needed to also prove that there are, in fact, Christian or Icelandic intellectuals.

There are still others who attempt to show that Wittgenstein sees Jewish thought in a negative light. In *Wittgenstein's Poker* Wittgenstein is charged with 'Jewish self-hatred, even anti-Semitism'.[29] We also find the suggestion that Wittgenstein's comment on the Jews thinking only 'reproductively' is a negative judgement.[30] More specifically, the 'notion that Jews think in a specific manner was bound into his constant self-torment, and he describes "Jewishness" (integrally part of him) as a limiting or distorting mechanism'.[31] This line of argument is also found in Monk's *Ludwig Wittgenstein: The Duty of Genius*. Monk correctly notes that Wittgenstein includes himself, along with Judaism, in the charge of being incapable of original thought, but Monk considers this to be 'absurd' in the light of Wittgenstein's great work:

> This belittling of his own achievement may have been a way of guarding himself from his own pride ... He was acutely aware of the dangers of false pride ... And it was against this background of such pride that he felt forced to remind himself of his limitations, of his 'Jewishness'.[32]

It is obvious that Monk regards Wittgenstein's understanding of his 'Jewishness' as a negative characteristic, and goes as far as considering Wittgenstein's statements about the lack of creativity amongst the Jews as a 'whole litany of lamentable nonsense'.[33] This inconsistency of recognizing the great thought of Wittgenstein and the Jewish people on the one hand, and Wittgenstein's allegedly negative critique on the other, is a false dichotomy. The reason for this confusion is based on a misunderstanding of Wittgenstein's appraisal of Jewish thought. The conception that Wittgenstein regards Jewish thought as substandard is tenuous and misses the complexity of Wittgenstein's thought and its relationship with Judaism (not to mention the obscure attempt to explain philosophy through psychological observations of false pride). Monk is correct to see a link between Wittgenstein and Jewish thought, but he sees this link as a contemptuous view.

In contrast to such a negative, and unfortunately common, opinion we can begin to see Wittgenstein's positive appraisal of Jewish thought by looking more closely at the remarks in *Culture and Value*. Wittgenstein writes,

> What Renan calls the '*bon sens precoce*' of the Semitic races (an idea which occurred to me too long ago) is their *unpoetic* mentality, which

heads straight for what is concrete. This is characteristic of my philosophy. Things are placed right in front of our eyes.[34]

Here it is possible to clip his remark and end up with a negative appraisal of Semitic races – 'their *unpoetic* mentality' – but it is obvious that this comment is not only directed towards Semitic thought, it is a comment on his own philosophy: 'This is characteristic of my philosophy. Things are placed right in front of our eyes.' His further comments add to his view on Jewish thought in relation to his own, and help us to see that it is not a negative evaluation:

It might be said (rightly or wrongly) that the Jewish mind does not have the power to produce even the tiniest flower or blade of grass; its way is rather to make a drawing of the flower or blade of grass that has grown in the soil of another's mind and to put it into a comprehensive picture.[35]

Amongst Jews 'genius' is found only in the holy man. Even the greatest of Jewish thinkers is no more than talented. (Myself for instance.) I think there is some truth in my idea that I really only think reproductively. I don't believe I have ever *invented* a line of thinking, I have always taken one over from someone else.[36]

It is typical for a Jewish mind to understand someone else's work better than he understands it himself.[37]

These quotations do not simply criticize Jewish thought, but they may be so construed by emphasizing the first half of each quotation and not following through his comments. Instead of our jumping to negative conclusions, we must see Wittgenstein's remarks as an important point about his own thought as well as Jewish thought. Rather than simply concluding that Wittgenstein has difficulties within Jewishness, we should try to understand what he is saying. We need to see what the relation is between non-productivity in one's own thought in conjunction with the comprehensive picture of others' thought, and what that relationship amounts to.

The non-creative aspect of both Hebraic thought and Wittgenstein's own is not a negative one. Instead, it is an important character of Wittgenstein's thought:

What we find out in philosophy is trivial; it does not teach us new facts, only science does that. But the proper synopsis of these trivialities is enormously difficult, and has immense importance. Philosophy is in fact the synopsis of trivialities.[38]

Furthermore, Wittgenstein says 'philosophical analysis does not tell us anything new about thought (and if it did it would not interest us)'.[39] Non-creativity is a fundamental aspect of Wittgenstein's thought, although he does admit to a bit of creativity – albeit possibly mistaken:

Incidentally, when I was in Norway during the year 1913–14 I had some thoughts of my own, or so at least it seems to me now. I mean I have the impression that at that time I brought to life new movements in thinking (but perhaps I am mistaken). Whereas now I seem to just apply old ones.[40]

Philosophy does not construct new buildings; rather, it takes the buildings at hand and organizes and clarifies them, while science does construct new buildings. In science we find the development of new theories for the structure of matter, new instruments for analysis of the universe; in short, there is a continual movement of construction and dismantling. In contrast, philosophy, as Wittgenstein says, 'leaves everything as it is'.[41] There are no creations as science might generate; instead, philosophy simply looks at the blueprints and perhaps clarifies or organizes them, but does not create them.

Both Jewish thought and Wittgenstein's thought follow a similar pattern of non-building. He states:

The faculty of 'taste' cannot create a new structure, it can only make adjustments to one that already exists. Taste loosens and tightens screws, it does not build a new piece of machinery. Taste makes adjustments. Giving birth is not its affair. I have taste. Even the *most refined* taste has *nothing* to do with creative power.[42]

In other words, while someone may construct a point of view and explain it in full detail, the Jewish mind may see how this particular viewpoint sits within other viewpoints, how it emerged, and where it may possibly lead. A glimpse of this is found in Wittgenstein's remark that 'it is typical for a Jewish mind to understand someone else's work better than he understands it himself'.[43] Perhaps it could be said that someone else's work is like a building in a city that has been carefully planned and fully understood by that person, while the Jewish mind sees not only the building, but also the city. This points to the positive evaluation of Jewish thought and Wittgenstein's thought, where buildings are not constructed in isolation, but the overall system is seen in its various forms. In effect, Wittgenstein sees the labyrinth of streets that is our language rather than one small section of a street that appears straight because of our short-sightedness. We can see that Wittgenstein associates his thought with Hebraic thought, rather than being anti-Semitic.

The Foreword of *Philosophical Remarks* yields further insight into the possible reason for the negative appraisal of Wittgenstein's comments on Jewish thought, and again, on close inspection, shows a positive evaluation of Jewish thought as well as a critique of creative system building. Wittgenstein comments:

> This book is written for such men as are in sympathy with its spirit. This spirit is different from the one which informs the vast stream of European and American civilization in which all of us stand. That spirit expresses itself in an onwards movement, in building ever larger and more complicated structures; the other in striving after clarity and perspicuity in no manner what structure. The first tries to grasp the world by way of its periphery – in its variety; the second at its centre – its essence. And so the first adds one construction to another, moving on and up, as it were, from one stage to the next, while the other remains where it is and what it tries to grasp is always the same.[44]

Now it is possible to see that Wittgenstein is not simply criticizing non-creative thinking. As a result, his discussion of Jewish thought as uncreative is actually compared favourably with his own thought; what he is critiquing is thought that is *not* in the Jewish style! Wittgenstein's thought, like Jewish thought, goes against the grain of the western tradition in which we stand. In contrast to this tradition, Wittgenstein and Jewish thought seek the substance, not the progress of creative structures. If we approach our study of Wittgenstein's thought from the aspect of Greek thought formerly discussed, then we may be led to think that non-creativity must be a negative appraisal. Just as Wittgenstein comments that 'in western civilization the Jew is always measured on scales that do not fit him',[45] so he himself is often measured by scales that do not fit. The work of Wittgenstein and Jewish thought lie in a region entirely different from most[46] because the prevalent western tradition is based on Greek thought.

The meaning of Wittgenstein's remark in its entirety, 'the Jew is a desert region, but underneath its thin layer of rock lies the molten lava of spirit and intellect',[47] takes on a new significance of positive evaluation for both Jewish thought and Wittgenstein. Wittgenstein, like the Jew, may appear as a desert region – uninterested in erecting systems on the ground, but permanently alive to the working of thought, and to the foundations that others build. Just as Wittgenstein's overview of others' work lies in his ability to enlighten them through the use of similes, metaphors and analogies, we can use an aspect of Hebraic thought as a fitting analogy for Wittgenstein's thought by his own admission. Wittgenstein rejects Greek thought and not, as commonly assumed, Jewish thought.

Hebraic thought as 'embodied'

In order to better understand the positive relation between Wittgenstein's and Hebraic thought, it is useful to first discuss the contrast between Greek and Hebraic thought (as understood in the early Judaic and Rabbinic tradition that was largely outside Greek influence). As was noted in the previous chapter, the Greek objective is to flee the complexity of the world and body to seek the unified intelligibility beyond the world (the foundation of meaning):

> It really has been shown to us that, if we are ever to have pure knowledge, we must escape from the body and observe things in themselves with the soul by itself. It seems likely that we shall, only then, when we are dead, attain that which we desire and of which we claim to be lovers, namely, wisdom ...[48]

This conception of knowledge places a primacy upon the soul in search of wisdom while the body, although not negated, is less consequential and significant in matters of knowledge. In other words, whatever significance Greek thought may place upon the corporeal and life experiences, it is ultimately the stable and definitive 'things in themselves' that yield 'pure knowledge'. In contrast, Kadushin notes that Hebraic thought 'is not speculative; it is organismic. Rabbinic ideas are not built up by ratiocination; they refer back directly to experience, and hence the integration of thought here is not a matter of design.'[49] The focal point of Hebraic thought is the corporeal; no consideration is given to the conceptual notions of 'pure knowledge' or 'things in themselves'. The source of authority and meaning is found in concrete practices for Hebraic thought, while Greek thought seeks the transcendent realm of abstract objects.

For the Hebrew the corporeal is better understood as integral to our being, rather than as a cloak that has a function but is ultimately to be removed. Instead, the Hebrew regards the person as a whole, without separating spirit and body. Berdyaev notes: 'The characteristic Platonic or Cartesian opposition of spirit and matter was alien to ancient Hebrew thought. For it, the living creature was the body.'[50] Rebecca Pentz also notes this distinction, where the

> core Judeo-Christian view of the soul is quite at odds with the views of Plato and Descartes. The word usually translated 'soul' comes from the word for breath, *nephesh*, and is used primarily to denote the whole living being. Far from being identified with consciousness or mental life, the *nephesh* can be hungry and thirsty. (Ps. 107:5)[51]

The Torah does not embrace dualistic concepts and never identifies the soul with the mind.[52] Likewise, the Rabbinic writings never use the terms 'spiritual' or 'material'.[53] The idea that our mind/soul, in contrast to our body, is the essence of our being which can perceive an intelligibility outside the world conflicts with Hebraic thought where, as Pentz notes, the soul 'eats and digests. It engages in sexual activities. So when the mind is irreversibly lost, Descartes' soul has left, Plato's soul has left, but Abraham's, Jacob's and Isaac's souls remain.'[54] Hebraic thought regards the body as the mode of existence; even if a person loses their thinking capacity, the core of the person remains, namely their living body.

Plato, however, thinks that by shunning the body we can gain unencumbered knowledge, which, of course, is best achieved when freed from the body.[55] The Greek pines for 'pure' reason, but the Hebrew is made of clay, learns from the clay, and will return to the clay.[56] Hebraic thought does not question the relation between body and soul since it does not distinguish between them. Indeed, the lack of inquiries within Hebraic thought regarding the distinction between body and soul leaves such discussions mute.[57] In effect, rather than debating questions of an ideal unified intelligibility beyond our world which the mind/soul might be able to perceive, the Hebrew's soul becomes thirsty, as it were, and looks for water.

Not only are the mind and soul unified with the body in Hebraic thought, but so is the fundamental element of the Hebrew religion, the Torah, 'embodied'. Unlike Platonic thought, where the goal is disembodiment to attain 'pure knowledge' of the Forms, Hebraic thought seeks 'embodied' knowledge of the Torah. The body is not merely an instrument of deception or a secondary principle, but is entwined with the Torah. While the Greek aspect of thought seeks foundations outside the world (such as the eternal Forms), which are thereby perceived by the mind/soul alone, the Hebrew sees the Torah as an earthly experience:

> The Torah must be ingested, become embodied, so that it is within the body, animating it. In some communities it was the custom on the first day of school to smear honey on a piece of paper on which was written the letters of the alphabet, to be eaten ... just as the prophet Ezekiel was commanded by God to eat the scroll (word) of God and fill his stomach and bowels with it.[58]

This view of the written text, the word, is far removed from abstract speculation. The words of the Torah are not intermediary signs that point to truth or reality; instead, they are ingested.[59] Indeed, the Torah and body are intertwined:

> R. Judah bar R. Simon taught that the Holy One, Blessed be He said: 'Within thy body are two hundred and forty-eight organs, and in the Torah are two hundred and forty-eight precepts [commandments]. If thou keepest the Torah, I shall keep thy body'.[60]

The human body requires the Torah, just as the Torah requires the human body; hence, the individual's body becomes the text and the text becomes the individual's body on a reciprocal basis.[61] Note that the Torah is like a living body. Since the Torah is understood as 'embodied', it is not surprising that the Torah scroll is treated as a body. For example, 'the congregation bow and kiss the body [Torah scroll], "dressed" as would be a king or high-priest, with silver breastplate, crown and ornaments, its waist tied by a garter belt'.[62] The Torah scroll is not only dressed as a body, it is also buried liked a body when worn out, and, conversely, a person's body is said to be buried like a Torah scroll.[63] This complementary relationship between the Torah and the body makes it clear that there is not an antecedent factor that determines meaning; rather, meaning is 'embodied' in the Hebrew's gut.[64] In the words of a Hebraic proverb, 'the body does not lie'.

Hebraic thought, then, is not simply abstract thought: the Torah itself is understood as 'embodied', and moreover, the practices of the Torah are understood as 'embodied' thought manifest through practice.[65] Once again, Hebraic thought seeks the concrete and does not subjugate it in favour of the transcendental. Sacha Stern notes that we should 'refer to Jewish identity not as a passive "experience" but rather as a *practice*'.[66] In the light of the emphasis on the practices of the Torah, we can find examples that clearly demonstrate the significance of the body for the Torah and meaning, in contrast to the metaphysical tendencies of Greek thought. The Torah as *mitzvot* (the practices of the people) are not abstract speculations – as if the *mitzvot* resemble, name, or point to higher principles – but are concrete activities. This strong link with practice is, so to speak, 'Jewish epistemology', where 'to know is to do'.[67] What is important are the activities on earth in contrast to speculations beyond the world; understanding is based in action, not contemplation. This is similar to Rhees's comment:

> The divinity of the Scriptures is not an 'objective fact' ... Once again: what do I recognise, when I recognise the divinity of the scriptures? And what sort of recognition is this? It is not *finding out something about them* – like discovering the date when they were written down. It is to live by them.[68]

The Hebrews live by the *mitzvot*. There is no development of a systematic or speculative rationale of their religion; rather, they concentrate on practice, the living of Torah.[69]

Simply doing what the Torah commands takes precedence over the confusion of contemplating what lies behind the Torah. The *mitzvot* are not imperfect representations of a conceptual ideal, nor do they point to the divine; they are the divine in action. In other words, Hebraic thought understands their God through the earthly and 'embodied' practice of the *mitzvot*, which are not hypotheses that link with God; rather, the practice and belief are one – it is God in the practice.[70] Rhees rightly observes:

> One's relation to God *is* the worship of God. ... if anyone should ask what the relation of the creature to God is, then one might most readily point to the worship of God, as if to say: 'Look there, you'll see.' And this is not the sort of thing that is suggested by Plato's idea of becoming as like to the divine as possible. You might even say it is the opposite. When Plato speaks of the form of the good ... he does not say that the sensible world, and earthly life, is any sort of imitation or likeness of that.[71]

The worship of God reflects the Hebrew's understanding of God, which in turn is not an abstract ideal, principally perceived by the soul, but an earthly relation.[72] The Hebrew knows God through the concrete practice and history of being a Hebrew, not through abstract speculations, and without necessitating questions of approximating an ideal.

In the light of the relational understanding between the Hebrews and their God as based on their practices and history, it should not be surprising that their God is understood in an earthly manner. Rhees says,

> I suppose this goes with the idea of the promises to Abraham by God as promises of an *earthy* redemption of his people. This notion of God as the God who had led this people out of Egypt, who had spoken to their prophets, etc., etc., is, I imagine, immensely important for the kind of religion they had and the importance they attached to the Scriptures.[73]

If we are discussing the role of the Hebrews' God in history, we are discussing concrete human affairs, not a static concept. Moreover, as Stern notes, 'God hardly ever appears in Rabbinic literature in isolation, as an object of independent discourse; He is always doing *something*, always part of some story in which He plays some role.'[74] It is the complex life of the Hebrews and their God that is informative, not a unified or simple foundation. The earthly understanding of the Hebrews' God lends itself to a humanizing tendency to which the Rabbis never objected.[75] Indeed, there is no evidence in Rabbinic sources of any opposition to anthropomorphism.[76] Hebraic thought sees the human characterization of God as a natural understanding of a relationship with their father. The Rabbis found that they needed to use the human character to represent God; indeed, 'a great number of scriptural passages ... represent nothing else but a record of a sort of *Imitatio hominis* on the part of God'.[77] Moreover, Heschel notes that 'there is something in the world that the Bible does regard a symbol of God. It is not a temple nor a tree, it is not a statue nor a star. The one symbol of God is *man*.'[78] The distinction between 'above' and 'below' has no bearing on Hebraic thought; hence, God resides amongst the people and is understood through their form of life.[79]

Shields, however, regards anthropomorphic understandings of God to be erroneous, and to 'compromise the dignity and sovereignty of the Deity'.[80] He views any humanizing of the Deity to be callow and to debase 'heaven bound' reason. Once again, the aspect of Greek thought discussed regards the complex and fleeting earthly activities as unable to secure knowledge, and thereby seeks the unified and unchanging knowledge behind the world. Likewise, according to Shields, God is not comprehensible in human terms, but is shown through Tractarian logic as the source of laws and logic.[81] Essentially, Shields's understanding of God is based on his conception of logical form; just as Plato's idea of God is based on his conception of the Good.[82] Since Shields bases his conception of God on conceptual categories, he misses the significance of the forms of life and falls under Heschel's critique:

> In their eagerness to avoid the possibility of ascribing anthropomorphic features to God, philosophers have traditionally adopted the procedure prevalent in general ontology, in which the notion of existence that served as a subject matter of analysis was derived from

the realm of inanimate rather than from the realm of animate and personal existence.[83]

To seek inanimate categories beyond the world is contrary to Hebraic thought and readily brings sceptical (philosophical) questions to bear: 'Does this meaning, image, word, etc., define reality?' or 'Is this the right God?' These divisions of thought are a Greek influence where, according to Kadushin, philosophical distinctions between body and soul, the incorporeality of God, etc.

> do violence ... to Rabbinic thought ... and show that when we employ the terms of classical philosophy even in an attempt to clarify rabbinic ideas, we are no longer within the rabbinic universe of discourse. Rabbinic statements about God arise as a result of interests entirely different from those of philosophic thought, represent human experiences that have nothing to do with speculative ideas.[84]

The Hebrews do not deduce that God must exist, like the idea that the perfect Triangle must exist behind the imperfect triangle, or that God must exist behind the Tractarian logic. Hebraic thought does not define God with conceptual categories such as the Good, logical form, omnipotence, etc.; rather, they see their God acting through history in human terms of love, anger, forgiveness, etc.[85] Hebraic thought is organismic and, as 'embodied', places life as the seat and limit of understanding God through human characterizations and practices.

Hebraic thought and Wittgenstein's later understanding of language

It is clear that Hebraic thought (as based in the Judaic tradition) finds authority and meaning in the concrete and practical; not in the transcendental and abstract. Therefore, Hebraic thought bears striking similarities to Wittgenstein's later conception of language in understanding language and theology (the grammar of religion) through our activities in the world. Neither posit a strict system of logic or a foundational realm; instead, there is a certain fluidity that results from looking at our application of language/practices, in contrast to a *theory* of language/theology. Monk rightly observes:

> Again and again in his lectures Wittgenstein tried to explain that he was not offering any philosophical *theory*; he was offering only the means to escape any *need* of such theory. The syntax, the grammar, of our thought could not be, as he had earlier thought, delineated or revealed by analysis – phenomenological or otherwise.[86]

Wittgenstein rejects the idea that there is a unified intelligibility that acts as a foundation, and about which a *theory* can be constructed to explain how it works. Equally, in Rabbinic Judaism, the idea of developing a theory about theology is rejected. Stern says,

> in the case of Rabbinic Judaism ... the well-known fact, indeed a virtual common place of Rabbinic Scholarship, [is] that the Rabbis eschewed any sort of systematic theology. They almost never formulated their religious beliefs in any organized way, let alone in a methodological discussion.[87]

What is being denied by Wittgenstein and Rabbinic Judaism is the idea of an extraordinary ability for a system to infer meaning while standing over language. In both cases the intent is to keep the focus on the actual use of words, or on the practices of being Jewish.

Instead of a system or *theory*, the process of Midrash (interpretation) is a way of engaging Rabbinic thought.[88] Bruns writes:

> Midrashic interpretation is not just something going on between a reader and a text with a view toward intellectual agreement between them. We need to get from under the model of a methodological solipsism that pictures a solitary reader exercising strategic power over a text.[89]

In contrast to explanatory systems, Midrash, according to Bruns, is not a system which enables us to perceive a unified intelligibility (such as the one form or essence of language and theology, or the common measure); indeed, he notes that 'the idea of speaking with one mind ('it is your

waters that we drink') is explicitly rejected'.[90] It is obvious that here is
a fluid and variable understanding to which the rabbis were open, and
therefore they did not consider interpretation to be a means to solve a
problem once and for all.[91] Indeed, meaning in Hebraic thought is never
complete and is thereby a process instead of a unified system.[92]

Likewise, for the later Wittgenstein, language cannot be cast into
a Tractarian type system of logic. Instead, language is more of a
convention;[93] that is, we agree in our use of language, and we do not find
the external system to judge language. Wittgenstein notes the significance
of our conventions in contrast to external absolutes:

> How should we get into conflict with truth, if our footrules were made
> of very soft rubber instead of wood and steel? – 'Well, we shouldn't get
> to know the correct measurement of the table.' – You mean: we should
> not get, or could not be sure of getting, *that* measurement which we get
> with our rigid rulers.[94]

Wittgenstein continually looks at the use and practice of language, not
an external logic, ideal Forms, etc. The rigid ruler does not measure the
truth; it measures the convention. Just as the Midrash is not a system
with which to procure the one correct answer, neither is Wittgenstein
interested in any system with determined rules that assume the 'correct'
answer lies outside our use of language.

This does not, however, imply a sort of indeterminate methodology
for Hebraic thought or for Wittgenstein. Stern states that 'multiple
interpretation in midrash bears little connection to the notion of indeterminacy'.[95] To say that there are infinite indeterminate meanings is
different than saying that there are multiple meanings, one distinction
being, for example, authority.[96] In Hebraic thought authority is understood in the sense that the oral and written Torah are spoken in the name
of God and the lineages of interpreters that follow, which then points to
the significance of the social aspect of authority, which is the acceptance
of the interpreters by the community.[97] Thus, as Bruns notes:

> In midrash authority is social rather than methodological and thus is
> holistic rather than atomic or subject-centered: the whole dialogue, that
> is the institution of midrash itself – rabbinic practice – is authoritative,

and what counts is conformity with this practice rather than correspondence to some external rule or theory concerning the content of
interpretation as such.[98]

In Rabbinic Judaism there is no absolute rule that determines the correct
interpretation; only the practice of being a Jew in a social setting can be
authoritative. Authority resides in the conventions and applications of
the language of theology where it is spoken and working, not in an ideal
realm that the language of theology attempts to emulate.[99] Neil Gillman
insightfully observes that 'it is not the Bible itself that retains primary
authority over what Jews believe and how Jews practise, but rather the
Bible is interpreted by tradition ... the center of authority is actually
removed from the Bible and placed in some *living body*'.[100] In Hebraic
thought meaning is not based on the one logic, be it logical syntax or
a meta-propositional point, but is based instead in the language-game
that is played. In other words, the point of Midrash is not to discover *the*
meaning, but to engage the text in the social context.[101] Hence, in the
Midrash 'each situation will command its own sense of how the text is to
be taken, which is why a legal text has to be open and loosely textured,
not indeterminate, but not a calculus of rules either'.[102] The point of
Midrash is an activity within the Jewish community, not an external
system or theory.

Once again, this understanding of the fluidity and importance of
social authority can be construed as opening the door to relativism and
indeterminancy. Schechter, for instance, comments that the 'Rabbis ...
show a carelessness and sluggishness in the application of theological
principles which must be most astonishing to certain minds which seem
to mistake merciless logic for God-given truths.'[103] This 'astonishment'
can be shown to be a quick judgement, particularly through a discussion
of a similar misunderstanding of Wittgenstein's thought. The assumed
problem of relativism in Hebraic or Wittgenstein's thought is based on
the yearning for generality, for the foundation that grounds meaning, and
upon the idea that language should mirror the essence of thought and
reality. The basic idea is that if meaning depends on application, then it is
arbitrary and no attention to the form of reality, or logic, is given. Rhees
rightly notes that Plato, for example, assumes that there must be a true
morality:

Apparently Plato thought there must be some reality to which a true morality would be adequate – in much the same sense as a true theory in astronomy be adequate to the real movements and distribution of the heavenly bodies. Otherwise he feared relativism and subjectivism; i.e. it seemed to him that morality, moral judgements, would be *arbitrary*.[104]

Stern notes a similar problem in modern studies of Judaism that favour 'either the scholarly article or the monograph, with them more fitting vehicles for Wissenschaft, the "science" of Judaism, with its claims to precise and comprehensive knowledge'.[105] It is often assumed that there must be a universal absolute that supports logic, morality or God, and once this is established it is imagined that we can progress without fearing relativism.

However, neither Wittgenstein's nor Hebraic thought, as a misplaced Greek perspective would posit, entail that everything goes or that all is relative simply because they reject external structures (Forms) to determine meaning. For example, there is no explanation for language itself, but there are explanations within the language-games. In other words, there may not be an absolute external measure to set the limits and definitions for language and meaning, but there are contextual measures. Wittgenstein writes:

The stream of life, or the stream of the world, flows on and our propositions are so to speak verified only at instants. Our propositions are only verified by the present. And so in some way they must be commensurable with the present; and they cannot be so *in spite of* their spatio-temporal nature; on the contrary this must be related to their commensurability as the corporeality of a ruler is to its being extended – which is what enables it to measure.[106]

Additionally, Monk comments,

Wittgenstein had many ways of characterising grammatical propositions – 'self-evident propositions', 'concept-forming propositions', etc. – but one of the most important was in describing them as *rules*. In emphasising the fluidity of the grammatical/material distinction, he was drawing attention to the fact that concept-formation – and thus

the establishing of rules for what it does and does not make sense to say
– is not something fixed by immutable laws of logical form (as he held
in the *Tractatus*) but is something that is always linked with a custom,
a practice.[107]

Wittgenstein does not subscribe to prescriptive rules, as those found
in formal calculi, but he does hold to the rules of the language-games.
Embodiment is what limits any hold of indeterminacy, primarily because
any thought will necessarily be found in practice and context. Wittgenstein
notes that following a rule is a 'practice' and a 'custom'; therefore, it is
not something that one individual can do – rules cannot be followed
privately.[108] Similarly, Peter Ochs says 'dislocation from the speech
community of Israel would imply dislocation from Torah, and, thereby,
from the possibility of meaningful speech and controlled behaviour'.[109]
Meaning is not determined by external Forms or structures, but it is not
an arbitrary private definition either; instead, meaning is governed in the
language-games (e.g. the speech community of Israel), where language
has its application.

Hebraic thought can be compared analogically with Wittgenstein's
remark, 'to imagine a language means to imagine a form of life'.[110]
Indeed, Bruns states that we must see Midrash as 'a form of life ...
rather than simply as a form of exegesis (in the technical sense); midrash
is concerned with practice and action'.[111] Midrash is not just doctrines,
concepts or a manner of speculation; rather, Midrash is concerned with
being Jewish.[112] And being Jewish is based in the earthly history and
practices of their people; as Wittgenstein notes, a religious belief is 'a
way of living'.[113] The Hebrews look towards their life of practices (i.e.
worship: sacrifice, prayer, etc.), not the logical structure 'behind' their
religion. Hebraic thought and Wittgenstein are interested in our human
activities and expressions, not in the common structure of bones underneath our flesh, or the external form of clothing that we must attempt
to emulate – as if meaning resides in a structure of bones or an ideal
fashion, while our humanness is a facade. This fluidity of thought, which
does not rest on absolutes or foundations, may yield dynamic meaning,
but as Louis Finkelstein correctly observes:

Opposing theological traditions had not given concern to the individual

Jew of earlier days because he had not supposed that Judaism was a 'system' of belief but, rather, of conduct. Action, based largely on impulse (which can never become a logical system, for it arises from a variety of human needs), is never free of apparent logical contradictions, and cannot be forced into a Procrustean bed of rational propositions.[114]

There was no formal system for the Rabbis, and no method was devised to censor Rabbinic thought's disregard of theological and logical consistency.[115] The relationship between the Jews and their God is comprised of their history and life, in contrast to a timeless unchanging truth or a rational analytical construction beyond their life experience and vision (i.e. their form of life). The result of looking at humanness, in contrast to an ideal, will not be, of course, a neat and clean system of thought like an anatomical drawing of an ideal skeleton, but will be a dynamic draft that is more closely related to human existence and our myriad forms.

It should be clear now that Hebraic thought offers an illuminating point of contact with Wittgenstein's thought, particularly as distinguished from Greek thought. The basis of this comparison rests on the mutual understanding of Wittgenstein's and Hebraic thought on the importance of an applied understanding, where the use of language, and the associated practices, are evidence of the reciprocal relation between language and logic. In other words, meaning is not a static ideal or object that must first be known and then carried to our applications of language. Instead, using language and the practices of the Israelites, for instance, *are* the basis for meaning, for understanding language (the grammar of religion), and for being an Israelite. Wittgenstein's thought is akin to Hebraic thought, but distinct from Greek thought, on this point: 'What has to be accepted, the given, is – so one could say – *forms of life*.'[116]

The problem of idols: the golden calf and philosophical confusion

The similar character of Wittgenstein's later philosophy and Hebraic thought, in contrast to Greek thought and Shields's, can be illuminated through the example of the Israelites and the golden calf. On the exodus from Egypt the Israelites, while waiting for the return of Moses from Mount Sinai, take their gold earrings, cast them into the form of a calf (a graven image), and worship with it.[117] This is, of course, a prime example of idolatry within a religious context, but it can be compared with idolatry in a philosophical context on an analogical basis. An idol, in religion and the philosophy of language, can be understood as that which is erroneously given meaning and authority (e.g. the golden calf and the simple object) and consequently leads to confusion. The problematic confusion that idols represent is a result of detaching religious ideas and language from their source of meaning and authority, namely, the form of life.

However, an understanding of the problem of idolatry, and consequently the treatment for idolatry, depend on whether it is viewed from a perspective that does pay attention to the form of life, or from a perspective that instead seeks a foundational meaning. For example, Shields's thought will be shown, like Greek thought, to emphasize foundational meaning. The problem of the golden calf, according to Shields, is that the Israelites are confused in thinking that the image of a calf is the 'ground of meaning'; on a similar basis as wrongly thinking that one's mental image of blue is the meaning of blue.[118] He thereby attempts to resolve the problem of idolatry as he would the mental image mechanism of meaning. That is, he wants to replace the golden calf and mental images with the 'ground of meaning' and pre-established conditions – just as Wittgenstein posits the simple object in the *Tractatus*, or Greek thought posits the Forms – to hold meaning fast and remove philosophical confusion.

Shields's understanding of the problem of the golden calf and his resolution for the problem – as based on his conception of language – neglects the Israelites' form of life and instead focuses on an abstract foundation. Ironically, although Shields rightly rejects the golden calf and the mental image mechanism of meaning, his 'solution' will be shown to be a philosophical idolatry.[119] In effect, he exchanges a religious idol for a philosophical idol (i.e. the 'ground of meaning'), and thereby furthers the confusion rather than clarifying it.

Rather than attempting to *resolve* the problems of the golden calf, or the philosophical confusion of thinking that abstract objects (e.g. simple object) hold meaning, by positing further external elements or idols such as the 'ground of meaning', Wittgenstein and Hebraic thought will be shown to *dissolve* these problems by turning to the form of life. This does not, of course, mean that the golden calf or abstract objects are acceptable. Hebraic thought and Wittgenstein reject the golden calf and abstract objects respectively, but they do not posit further idols to resolve the problems – they destroy idols.

For example, the later Wittgenstein rejects the ideas that philosophical confusions are a result of language not connecting to the simple object and that the confusions can be solved by understanding the underlying logical syntax. The problem of determining the connection between language and the underlying simple object is dissolved when he turns to descriptions of how language connects to the language-games in the form of life. Likewise, Hebraic thought will be shown to reject the golden calf (like the simple object) since it displaces the Israelites' form of life as the basis for meaning and authority and exchanges it for an inanimate static object.

The example of the golden calf provides an analogy for Wittgenstein's conception of confusion in language within a religious context. In both cases, philosophical and religious, idols represent an abstraction of authority and meaning from concrete and normative practices and consequently lead to further confusion. The meaning language has is not based on a transcendental realm of abstract objects; likewise, within Hebraic thought neither God nor the meaning of religious ideas are based in an idol. In order to clarify the confusion of idols the treatment is found, as Wittgenstein continually emphasizes in his later thought, in the concrete and practical applications of language, not the idols of metaphysical theories. Shields agrees with Wittgenstein's remark, 'all that philosophy can do is destroy idols'; however, he misses the significance of the word 'all' and the latter half of Wittgenstein's remark, 'and that means not creating a new one'.[120] Instead of positing further idols like Shields's 'ground of meaning' in an attempt to resolve confusion, Wittgenstein and Hebraic thought, in their respective fields, will be shown to dissolve idols by turning to the form of life.

Shields's treatment of idols

Shields's conception of the confusion of idols and the required treatment in philosophical and religious contexts is set in his conception of language which is, once again, similar to the early Wittgenstein and foundational Greek thought. For instance, if we can see the structure behind language, the elements of the proposition which link with the web of logical space, then we have sense and meaning while the context of a proposition loses application. There is a logical priority given to the inherent sense of a word and the object with which it links, over the context and use of a proposition. This aspect of Wittgenstein's early work carries a certain Greek understanding as shown in the third chapter, namely, that there is a foundation of meaning that functions independently of our applications of language in the world.

Shields has an affinity with this early Wittgensteinian and Greek style of thought as is shown in his approval of Ackermann's conception of meaning:

> Both logic and grammar must be given completely in advance, or the horizons of one-step hermeneutics would not already exist in order to fix clear meaning. Meaning is determinate because it is created by such structures and not by exploration of the world. There is a structure in language that can be known in advance.[121]

It is clear that Shields thinks grammar is antecedent to our use of language, that there is a fixed meaning that we can *know* in advance. Any notion of a structure known in advance can only be perceived by the mind/soul, since it would be impossible to actually see elements of this structure from within a worldly perspective. For example, who can see the Platonic Forms or a simple object? Shields approaches the example of the golden calf in this Greek and Tractarian manner. He assumes that there is a 'ground of meaning' that determines meaning, and that this 'ground of meaning' is not 'something' in the fleeting world; indeed, to assume it is 'something' in the world 'threatens' the 'ground of meaning'.[122] According to Shields, a golden calf is merely an object in the world; it is unable to sustain the Israelites and cannot provide meaning.[123]

Shields is, of course, right to question the value of the golden calf;

however, it is important to note that he frames the problem within his conception of the 'ground of meaning'. The problem with his argument is that he removes significance from the form of life which does provide the context for meaning and authority, and replaces it with an abstract 'ground of meaning'. This problem can be shown through Shields's interpretation of the problem of mental images and meaning alongside the problematic golden calf. Indeed, Shields interprets the problem of the idol within the framework of the problem of mental images in semantics since he regards the golden calf to be the equivalent of a mental image.[124]

The basic problem of placing a mental image as the foundation of meaning begins with questioning how words connect with reality. The word 'blue', for instance, does not really contain, so to speak, 'Blueness'. Since the word does not contain 'Blueness', we turn to a mental image which, it is thought, must copy 'Blueness', perhaps from memories of a chart. Then, when requested to pick a blue ball, we can compare our mental image of blue with each ball until the blue ball is selected. The trouble with this idea of a mental image as the foundation for meaning is that it does not resolve any difficulties since there is still the problem of how we gained the mental image of blue in the first place, and how accurate it is. If the use of the word 'blue' is thought to lack a ground of meaning, then how can the mental image of blue have a ground? We may think we are getting closer to the real understanding of blue, but all that has happened is that the problem of trying to understand how the word 'blue' can be connected with the colour blue, becomes the problem of how the mental image of blue can be connected with the colour blue. No matter how many intermediaries we have, we will always need another, leading to an infinite regress.

Shields's application of the confusion of thinking that mental images hold meaning to the Israelites and the golden calf runs as follows: since a proposition does not 'contain' God, so to speak, Shields thinks that the Israelites turn to a mental image, such as a calf, whereby it is then assumed that God is found in the image. According to Shields, the Israelites lost faith in the unseen God and made an idol according to a mental image of God, and just as it is a mistake to think that meaning resides in a mental image semantically, so it is a mistake to think there is any meaning in the idol.[125] The problem is placed squarely in thinking that the 'ground of meaning' (i.e. God) can be a mental image and, perhaps even more erroneously, can be a visible object in the world. Shields appears to take Calvin's line of thought: 'The god whom man has thus conceived inwardly he attempts to embody outwardly. The mind in this way, conceives the idol ... on which they imagined that God was visibly depicted to their eyes.'[126] Shields thinks that the Israelites are philosophically confused because they assume that the 'ground of meaning' (i.e. God) can be a mental image and fashioned into a visible object that holds meaning, while instead it actually 'threatens the ground of meaning'.[127]

It is easy to agree with Shields: mental images do not sustain meaning, it is difficult to imagine how a golden calf could sustain anyone, and the Israelites were not to worship with graven images in any case. But our quick agreement with Shields's conclusion can cloud the recognition of potential problems in his argument. Shields correctly notes that the golden calf and mental images do not support meaning, but he wrongly thinks that the 'ground of meaning' does. The problem with Shields's method is that he looks past the form of life – which does provide meaning – to an abstract foundation. His solution to the problem of the mental image mechanism for meaning and the golden calf is to turn to the 'ground of meaning' (i.e. God).[128] It is clear that Shields's understanding of language and meaning conforms with his conception of meaning in a religious context.

Not only does Shields wrongly posit a 'ground of meaning'(rather than the form of life) as fundamental to the problem of idols and their resolution, he also inappropriately forces a philosophical theory onto the Israelites. Shields is correct to note the confusion in regarding mental images as sustaining meaning, as if meaning resides in a mental image alone, but it is questionable to use the same method and resolution to analyse the Israelites' God and the golden calf. Shields argues that (a) the Israelites were wrong to make an idol since (b) mental images are not the foundation of meaning. Once again, he is right about both points taken in isolation, but it is questionable to claim that the Israelites' fault is best understood in terms of the problem of mental images. Moreover, Shields's framing of the golden calf problem in terms of the mental image mechanism of meaning can lead us to misunderstand the Israelites. The Israelites were not so naive as to think that their God really looks like a calf, and they are not creating faulty philosophical theories based on the mental image mechanism of meaning. If the Israelites think of the golden calf in the same manner as the mental image mechanism of meaning, then perhaps they actually thought that their image of a calf was the best image of God – particularly if the left back leg had been a bit longer. This is clearly not the case.

In the case of the blue ball, if someone said it was red, then perhaps we could change their ways by showing them the accepted use of the word 'blue'. However, it is hard to imagine someone trying to show the Israelites that their God, for example, looks more like a fish than a calf. Wittgenstein observes that we can show people their errors, and they may change their ways, but in the case of religious practices we are not testing hypotheses to see which come closer to the 'truth': 'This is not how it is in connexion with the religious practices of a people; and what we have here is *not* an error.'[129] Rather than saying that the image of a calf or a fish are equally wrong when applied to God, we could, in a sense, say they are equally right. In other words, if the Israelites had used the image of a fish instead of a calf, it would not have been a less accurate depiction of their God. There may be a representative object for the word 'blue', but there is no object that depicts God. Wittgenstein notes that God is one of the earliest words learned, but 'I wasn't shown [that which the picture pictured].'[130]

Meaning is not a result of 'calling-up' the correct image, as if we understand a word simply by being shown the correct image, and God in particular cannot be understood by means of 'calling-up' the image of a calf. It is questionable to place the confusion of thinking that the mental image of blue holds the meaning of blue upon the Israelites, where the image of a calf is thought to hold the meaning of their God. Wittgenstein realizes that the 'misunderstanding of the logic of language (or the way language functions) gives rise to metaphysics', such as the mental image mechanism of meaning, but he 'would not call an ancient ritual practice "metaphysics"'.[131] The Israelites are not philosophers who reach the opinion that the image of a golden calf holds the meaning of their God, and they are not interested in analysing the concept of the golden calf philosophically. Shields is correct to reject the mental image mechanism for meaning and the golden calf, but he inappropriately places the problem of the former on the latter.

For example, we do not think that William Blake's image of God, *Ancient of Days*, holds the meaning of God, or that it is an accurate depiction of God. And we do not think that Michelangelo's painting, *The Creation of Adam*, depicts God anymore accurately than Blake's does. Wittgenstein notes that 'we certainly wouldn't think this the Deity. The picture has to be used in an entirely different way if we are going to call the man in that queer blanket "God".'[132] Michelangelo would not think he had actually depicted how God looks; instead, there is a different way of using such a picture.[133] What makes the image of God a representation of God is not simply a pictorial nature. Michelangelo's painting of God is not able to explain God by means of the colours and brush strokes alone. We cannot understand the Christian's God by looking at the ceiling of the Sistine Chapel; rather, we need to look at the practices and language of those in the Sistine Chapel (i.e. their form of life).

The point here is not that the Israelites view the golden calf in the same manner that Michelangelo views his painting. Instead, the importance of the form of life must be highlighted for our understanding of the Israelites and their God, and for Michelangelo and his God. Moreover, when Michelangelo painted God, and when the Israelites formed the calf, they already understood their God in context; the image was not, so to speak, the creation of their God. The images supplement the text of Michelangelo's life with his God and the Israelites' life with their God; the images do not lead to the text of their lives. For example, the Israelites call their God *Yahweh* before and after Moses ground the golden calf to dust; their God was not ground to dust, only the tool of worship was destroyed.[134] Moreover, it is hard to imagine that the Israelites thought that the calf they had just made from their earrings had brought them out of Egypt – a chronological distortion – or that it was the most accurate depiction of their God on the basis of the mental image mechanism of meaning. Wittgenstein notes that 'we don't wonder whether the picture is the thought or the meaning, we simply *use* pictures, sentences and so on'.[135] The Israelites used the golden calf to express their worship of the God who had brought them out of Egypt. The golden calf was subsequently destroyed, but the God they worshipped remained. The Israelites' base the meaning of the word 'God' on their living history with that God, not on the mental image of a calf.

It is misguided to assume that the Israelites have a mental image of their God that is functionally equivalent to the philosophical confusion of thinking a mental image of blue holds the meaning of blue. However, it is senseless to offer the 'ground of meaning' as the solution to the problems of the mental image mechanism for meaning and the golden calf. Once again, this does not mean that the golden calf is acceptable. Instead, it means that the mental image mechanism of meaning is not a constructive context for discussions of the problem of the golden calf. It is important to note, however, that just because it cannot be 'proved' that the Israelites are wrong to worship with the golden calf on the basis of the confused mental image mechanism of meaning, it does not follow that it is impossible to conclude that the Israelites are wrong. In other words, just because Shields's case against the Israelites and the golden calf is questionable, it does not follow that the Israelites are without fault. Rather, the golden calf can only be understood – for or against – within its religious context (not as set against the 'ground of meaning'). What *does* provide meaning, in contrast to idols and the 'ground of meaning', is the Israelites' form of life.

Shields's conception of confusion and consequently his treatment for confusion, in both philosophical and religious contexts, follows a Tractarian basis and thereby focuses on transcendental foundations. He inappropriately places meaning and authority in abstract realms which are no less confused than the mental image mechanism for meaning and other idols which do not hold meaning in any concrete sense. It is equally difficult to understand Shields's 'ground of meaning' and pre-established conditions as it is to understand the Tractarian simple objects – both of which are stipulations to hold meaning fast, but are incredibly difficult, if not impossible, to grasp. The problem is that Tractarian simples, the mental image mechanism of meaning, and the 'ground of meaning', detach meaning and authority from the form of life. Therefore, by using Shields's approved definition of idolatry – 'idolatry refers to objects of ultimate trust or confidence that do not and cannot bear the weight of reliance that we place on them for providing sustenance and meaning'[136] – we find that his theory also falls into idolatry. In effect, Shields uses a philosophical idol as a treatment for religious idols. Moreover, the depth of the problem is not seen through such an analysis. To imagine that the golden calf was used by the Israelites as an ostensive definition for their God, as is found in the mental image mechanism of meaning, misses the nature of the problem and the significance of the form of life for its dissolution.

A Hebraic and Wittgensteinian treatment of idols

The golden calf provides an example of confusion within a religious context that is analogical to Wittgenstein's later conception of confusion within the philosophy of language. In the case of the golden calf, the confusion is not simply an erroneous image, but is a grievous distortion of the Israelites' form of life (i.e. their theology and practices which reveal their understanding of their God). In effect, by using a golden calf in their worship the Israelites are rejecting the authority and meaning of their theology and practices which is tantamount to rejecting their God. It will be shown that the golden calf is detached from their form of life and thereby is a practice of idolatry, and that the treatment is not to search for 'better' idols, but is to destroy the idols of confusion (e.g. Shields's 'ground of meaning', golden calf).

The destruction of idols does not, however, mean that there is no representation of God, as Shields assumes. His Calvinist basis influences his discussion of the golden calf. For example, Calvin writes that the basic problem of an idol is that 'nothing [is] more incongruous than to reduce the immense and incomprehensible Deity to the stature of a few feet'.[137] In other words, it is an obvious contradiction for the finite to contain the infinite so there is no need to even discuss any particular religious context.[138] It is thought that any notion of the 'ground of meaning' being visible in the world is erroneous. The fact that this conception misses the importance of the Israelites' form of life – as the basis for understanding the confusion of the golden calf, and for understanding their God – is a fundamental distinction between Shields and Hebraic thought. The Israelites' form of life (i.e. their practices and theology) is the basis for rejecting the calf as a confused practice (idolatry), and *is* representative of their God.

Hebraic thought and Wittgenstein's later philosophy similarly focus on the form of life as essential for authority and meaning and reject abstract speculations. Heschel says:

> Ontology inquires: what is *being*? What does it mean to be? The religious mind ponders: what is *doing*?' Moreover, 'it would be futile … to explore the meaning of music and abstain from listening to music. It would be just as futile to explore the Jewish thought from a distance, in self-detachment. Jewish thought is disclosed in Jewish living.[139]

If we attempt to find meaning in Judaism through questions of a detached nature, then the result is confusion. Indeed, the 'Hebrew Bible is not a book about heaven – it is a book about earth'.[140] There is no theory or speculative rationale of their religion; rather, there are the concrete practices, the living of Torah.[141] Accordingly, Arthur Hertzberg writes, 'the emphasis of Jewish faith is therefore neither on metaphysical speculation nor on dogma but on human action'.[142] The source of authority and meaning for religious ideas within Hebraic thought are their concrete practices within their form of life.

Wittgenstein also places the form of life as essential for meaning and authority. He continually wants to understand the connection between logic and reality but, in contrast to earlier attempts that posit the elementary proposition, he gives up the idea of formal concepts. Wittgenstein turns from his earlier view that logic is a formal structure underlying language to sustain meaning, to logic being formed through our use of language. Dilman correctly notes that in the

> *Tractatus* language is the tail which logic, as the top-dog, wags. In the *Investigations* this is reversed: 'language-games' involve our behaviour, they are organically interrelated, and form an important, indeed, inseparable part of human life, and logic appears in that. It does not have an independent anchor outside or separate from it.[143]

If language does not stem from an *a priori* structure, then it must be embedded in and arise from the 'life' of language. Wittgenstein says, 'what is called "language" is something made up of heterogeneous elements and the way it meshes with life is infinitely various'.[144] Language and logic are understood through the life and context within which we use language, but without either being first; they are reciprocal. In a sense, formal concepts, ideal Forms, and logical form as that which informs meaning, switch to the forms of life, where life becomes the significant factor of understanding logic in contrast to some rational notion of the *a priori*.

The practices and history of language are the concrete source of authority and meaning in language; as Wittgenstein says, 'God grant the philosopher insight into what lies in front of our eyes.'[145] If we do not pay attention to language applications and instead speculate upon words and concepts detached from the form of life, then what are we left with? Once again, Wittgenstein writes: 'Is it, as it were, a contamination of the sense that we express it in a particular language which has accidental features, and not as it were bodiless and pure?'[146] Additionally: 'We are talking about spatial and temporal phenomena of language, not about some non-spatial, non-temporal phantasm.'[147] What language rests upon is not a transcendental structure of abstract objects or an ideal foundation, but a changing form of life. Indeed, Wittgenstein says: 'To imagine a language is to imagine a form of life.'[148]

Wittgenstein's later understanding of language and Hebraic thought have an analogical view of the importance of the concrete and practical applications of language and religion respectively. For example, in the case of language, confusion is a result of detaching meaning and authority from the applications of language and instead emphasizing transcendental objects. In the religious example of the golden calf, confusion is a result of the Israelites using an object (i.e. the golden calf) that is detached from their established practices. In both cases, philo-sophical and religious, an object (e.g. simple object, golden calf) is posited that does not hold meaning or authority. Schechter notes that idols are representative of 'every separation from God, though not with the intention of sin, but with the purpose of establishing an intermediary, is, as we see, considered as setting up another God'.[149] The idols of religion, and those of philosophy, are erroneous intermediaries that are thought to hold meaning and authority but, by taking the place of that which does hold meaning and authority (i.e. the form of life), they actually advance confusion.

Wittgenstein similarly notes that within the philosophy of language there is a 'tendency to assume a pure intermediary between the proposi-tional signs and the facts. Or even to try to purify, to sublime, the signs themselves. – For our forms of expression prevent us in all sorts of ways from seeing that nothing out of the ordinary is involved, by sending us in pursuit of chimeras.'[150] In religious and philosophical contexts an idol represents an object (or theory) that is outside contexts of application and consequently leads to confusion.

Accordingly, the golden calf is an erroneous object within the Israelites' practice of worship since their theology stipulates that graven images are not acceptable: 'You shall not make a graven image for yourself.'[151] The confusion of the idol is not simply a result of the fact that their God does not look like a calf; more importantly, the use of graven images and idolatry are not appropriate practices in their form of life. For example, Heschel writes:

> According to an ancient belief, the prophet Elijah, 'the angel of the covenant', is present whenever the act of circumcision is performed. To concretize that belief, a vacant chair, called 'Elijah's chair', is placed near the seat of the *sandek* (god-father). This is the limit of representation: a vacant chair. To place a picture or a statue of the prophet on it, would have been considered absurd as well as blasphemous.[152]

Surely, the problem with placing a picture of the prophet Elijah on the chair is not that someone will think that it is Elijah, but that it is not an accepted practice. If someone did think the picture was Elijah, then not only would it be rather bizarre, it would also be difficult to know how to show this person that the picture is not Elijah. A similar understanding can apply to the golden calf, the problem is not simply that the Israelites actually thought their God resembles a calf;[153] rather, the problem is that it was a practice that is a transgression against their theology and established practices which *are* representative of their God.[154]

The golden calf is not an image of the Israelites' God, but it is wrong to assume that there is no image for the Israelites to look at, and that the answer to the problem is to turn from the golden calf to an abstract and unseen 'ground of meaning' as the basis for authority and meaning.[155] The core problem of an idol within Hebraic thought is that it makes one look to the *wrong* representation of their God. The representation of Elijah is not a picture, but is the covenant (and associated practices), and the representation of God is not a golden calf, but is the Israelites' form of life.[156] The Israelites that worship with the golden calf are confused in thinking that they *have* a symbol of their God; on the contrary, they *are* the symbol. Heschel says, 'there is something in the world that the Bible does regard a symbol of God. It is not a temple nor a tree, it is not a statue nor a star. The one symbol of God is man.'[157] This does not simply mean, of course, that any one human is independently the symbol of God; rather, it is the community of Israelites and their practices that are to be holy and the symbol of God.[158]

Hebraic thought's emphasis on the concrete practices of the community in contrast to independent symbols is apparent in Heschel's remark: 'what is necessary is not to *have a symbol but to be a symbol*. In this spirit, all objects and all actions are not symbols in themselves but ways and means of enchaining the living symbolism of man.'[159] It is a confusion to assume that there is one symbol of God, instead the community of the Israelites is the 'living' symbol comprised of their practices and history. Thus, 'beyond the idea of the imitation of divinity goes the conviction of the divinity of deeds. Sacred acts, mitzvot, do not only imitate; they represent the Divine.'[160] Likewise, it is a confusion to assume that a simple object, as an independent element, connects language to and underlying logical syntax to provide meaning. God is not represented or understood by means of an independent object, and language is not understood by means of independent objects. Wittgenstein's later understanding of language rejects an atomistic structure built from a simple object to complex propositions, and instead shows that there is an entire system of language right before us. Language does not mirror an underlying logical syntax; rather, it is developed within the form of life (culture).[161]

In Wittgenstein's later understanding of language there is no underlying structure or idol that determines meaning. He notes:

> Philosophers very often talk about investigating, analysing, the meaning of words. But let's not forget that a word hasn't got a meaning given to it, as it were, by a power independent of us, so that there could be a kind of scientific investigation into what the word really means. A word has the meaning someone has given it.[162]

Rules are not established by an immutable logical form, but are formed through practices within a culture.[163] Likewise, the Torah is in a reciprocal relationship with the practices of the Israelites: 'Torah and Mitzvoth are a complement to each other, or, as a Rabbi expressed it, "they borrow from each other".'[164] Indeed, the written Torah is not conclusively more authoritative than are practices and social authority: 'the rabbinic enactments are Torah, and in a certain respect are "more weighty" than the laws of the written Torah'.[165] Concrete practices are an integral component of meaning for Wittgenstein's later conception of language and Hebraic thought.

The dynamic relation between the Torah and Israel obviously does not mean that 'anything goes' (the golden calf is rejected); rather, meaning is based in their history, tradition and social authority.[166] Bruns writes:

> In midrash authority is social rather than methodological and thus is holistic rather than atomic or subject-centered: the whole dialogue, that is the institution of midrash itself – rabbinic practice – is authoritative, and what counts is conformity with this practice rather than correspondence to some external rule or theory concerning the content of interpretation as such.[167]

Likewise, Wittgenstein notes that following a rule is a 'practice' and a 'custom'; therefore, it is not something that one individual can do – rules cannot be followed privately.[168] Meaning is not determined by external Forms or structures, but it is not an arbitrary private definition either; rather, the source of meaning is the application of language within the form of life.

The close relationship between the Israelites' form of life and their God is marked by their holiness. Schechter says, 'in its broad features holiness is another word for *Imitatio Dei*, a duty intimately associated with Israel's close contact with God. The most frequent name of God in the Rabbinic literature is "the Holy One," occasionally also "Holiness," and so Israel is called holy.'[169] The Israelites are holy and representative of their God, and to remain a representation they are to be set apart from that which is not holy.[170] The distinction between what is holy, and what is not holy, is made concrete within their form of life. That is, their religious practices are distinct and identify them with their God, while foreign practices (such as the use of a calf image) represent a confusion. This is analogical to the fact that words can belong within a particular language-game, so using them outside their language-game results in confusion.

In the example of the golden calf, the Israelites step outside their established practices and, so to speak, their language-game. They 'made a calf in Horeb [Sinai], and fell down before the cast image; and they changed their glory into the image of an ox eating grass'.[171] The glory that the Israelites changed was that of their form of life and holiness (*Imitatio Dei*) for that of a static golden calf. Shields, although he rightly rejects the golden calf, exchanges the glory of the Israelites' form of life for a philosophical idol (i.e. the 'ground of meaning'). Likewise, philosophers often exchange the form of life for idols (e.g. intermediaries, theories).

Exchanging a form of life for the confusion of idols in religious and philosophical contexts can be likened to an illness.[172] The importance of clarity within the philosophy of language, and holiness within Hebraic thought, certainly implies that a distortion of either is problematic. Once again, Wittgenstein says, 'the philosopher's treatment of a question is like the treatment of an illness'.[173] And Schechter says, 'it is especially the Torah which is considered the best remedy against the Evil *Yezer* [imagination]'.[174] The problems of conceptual confusions within philosophy, and the Evil *Yezer* (which tempts the Israelites to worship with the golden calf) within Hebraic thought, are not indicative of cursory mistakes, but are deeply ingrained illnesses within our conception of language and the human condition respectively. For example, the Rabbis consider idolatry to be a madness[175] that is 'more deeply rooted in the nature of man than any other passion'.[176] The serious problem of the Israelites' use of the golden calf separates them from holiness (i.e. *Imitatio Dei*) and thereby disfigures their community and their land.[177]

Wittgenstein regards problems within philosophy to be similarly deep: 'The problems arising through a misinterpretation of our forms of language have the character of *depth*. They are deep disquietudes; their roots are as deep in us as the forms of our language and their significance is as great as the importance of our language.'[178] For example, creating theories that posit intermediaries (e.g. mental image mechanism of meaning) to explain what should be a matter of common sense betrays confusion. As mentioned previously, to think that the meaning of 'blue' can be explained by means of a mental image of blue is a superficial explanation that only furthers the confusion. The abundance of philosophical theorizing – like the madness of heeding to the Evil *Yezer* and worshipping with a golden calf – may have led Wittgenstein to remark: 'In life we are surrounded by death, so too in the health of our intellect we are surrounded by madness.'[179] To be caught in the madness of idols, philosophical or religious, leads to confusion and requires a remedy.

The illnesses of being separated from holiness and of being confused philosophically are not treated by Hebraic thought or Wittgenstein's later philosophy by creating improved idols or theories. Nevertheless, Wittgenstein's early thought did maintain a certain sense of the immutability of logical form that could determine language. As discussed above, his early philosophy is, in a sense, similar to an aspect of Greek thought that tends to place an ideal realm of foundational meaning beyond our particular form of life, and leaves us responsible to make certain that our concepts link with this 'reality' (e.g. Platonic Forms or the web of logical form). The temptation to see 'beyond' the complexity of life to determine how meaning fits together (the structure of language) is, however, criticized by the later Wittgenstein: 'For they see in the essence, not something that already lies open to view and that becomes surveyable by a rearrangement, but something that lies beneath the surface.'[180] Similarly, within Hebraic thought, Heschel says we fail to understand God 'not because we do not know how to extend our concepts far enough, but because we do not know how to begin close enough'.[181] Neither Wittgenstein's later philosophy nor Hebraic thought are metaphysical *theories*, nor do they construct theories (idols). In contrast to such metaphysical temptations, the treatment is to destroy idols and look to the established activities within a form of life as the source of meaning and authority.

Certainly we cannot say that Wittgenstein's thought informs Hebraic thought, nor does Hebraic thought inform Wittgenstein's thought, but we can say that there is an interesting analogy between the two. God's command not to use graven images is not a *theory* about their God for the Israelites, but instead directs their attention to their practices in their form of life. If the Israelites look to the golden calf or to abstract theories for an understanding of their God, then they are led to confusion. Instead, the source of meaning and authority are their theology and associated practices, which *are* representative of their God. Likewise, Wittgenstein's critique of philosophical idols (e.g. simple object, ideal Forms, etc.) is not a philosophical attempt to find the right *theory* for language, but instead directs the philosophers attention to the concrete forms of life. If a philosopher seeks the meaning of a word solely in the object to which it refers, the underlying logical syntax or a transcendental realm of abstract objects, then confusion will follow.

Hebraic thought shows that when the Israelites look to their form of life, instead of a static idol, they show that they understand their God, and Wittgenstein shows that when philosophers look to the form of life, instead of fabricating philosophical idols, they show that they understand language.

Endnotes

1 Winch, 'Discussion of Malcolm's Essay', 109.
2 Once again, Drury states: 'Origen taught that at the end of time there would be a final restitution of all things. That even Satan and the fallen angels would be restored to their former glory.' 'Conversations with Wittgenstein' (161). Origen's idea of *apokatastasis* (re-establishment) denotes that, through time, all return to God: 'The end is always like the beginning.' *De Principiis*, I, vi, 2. The implication is an ultimate return to an incorporeal existence in God in spite of our practices.
3 Drury, 'Conversations with Wittgenstein', 161.
4 In addition, Fergus Kerr states: 'If the notes in *Culture and Value* are anything to go by, Wittgenstein has a strong sense of his Jewishness.' *Theology After Wittgenstein* (Oxford: Basil Blackwell, 1986), 35. Furthermore, Albert Levi considers Wittgenstein's inclination in religion to be Judaic and concrete. 'The Biographical Sources of Wittgenstein's Ethic', *Telos*, 38 (Winter 1979), 75.
5 The diversity of Jewish thought can be highlighted by noting a contrast between the strand of Jewish thought selected and an aspect of medieval Jewish philosophy. For example, Moses Maimonides says, in *The Guide for the Perplexed*, that his purpose is to 'address those who have studied philosophy and have acquired sound knowledge, and while firm in religious matters are perplexed and bewildered on account of the ambiguous and figurative expressions employed in holy writings'. Moses Maimonides, *The Guide for the Perplexed*, trans. M. Friedländer (New York: Dover Publications, 1961), 5. Maimonides addresses the apparent discrepancy between the logic of Aristotelian philosophy and the chaotic nature of the theology of classical Judaism (e.g. Talmudic commentaries). In short: he 'sought to impose a unified and definitive view ... [that] had previously been anathema in the

Jewish community'. Oliver Leaman, *Moses Maimonides* (New York: Routledge, 1990), 6.

6 Louis Finkelstein, introduction to Schechter, *Aspects of Rabbinic Theology*, xvi. Abraham Heschel notes that 'it is of extreme importance that theology should endeavour to operate with the categories indigenous to the insights of theology instead of borrowing its categories from speculative philosophy or science'. Abraham Heschel, *The Prophets* (New York: Harper & Row, 1962), 265. Moreover, part of the distinction between Hebraic thought in the Judaic tradition and later forms of thought outside Judea is a result of the continued use of the Hebrew language in Judea. Indeed, Leaman notes, 'it would have been difficult for Maimonides to write his philosophical works in Hebrew given the paucity of philosophical tradition in that language, whereas Arabic provided a friendly medium for both scholarly and ordinary debate'. Leaman, *Moses Maimonides*, 14.

7 A forerunner of Maimonides is Solomon Ibn Gabirol whose work, *The Fountain of Life*, is regarded by Theodore James as lacking influence within Jewish contexts since its 'neo-platonic linguistic structures' make it apparently non-Jewish. Theodore E. James, introduction to *The Fountain of Life*, by Solomon Ibn Gabirol (New York: Philosophical Library, 1962), n.p.

8 Finkelstein, introduction to *Aspects of Rabbinic Theology*, xviii. It is interesting to note that Wittgenstein writes: 'in order to be able to live and work I must not allow any foreign goods (i.e. philosophical goods) to enter my consciousness'. Letter to von Wright (21 February 1947). 'Letters to von Wright', *Cambridge Review*, 28 February, 1983.

9 Finkelstein, introduction to *Aspects of Rabbinic Theology*, xviii.

10 Kadushin, *The Rabbinic Mind*, 337. Kadushin also observes that 'rabbinic dogmas are vastly different from the dogmas of medieval Jewish theology. The rabbinic dogmas do not constitute a creed, and they even permit, in some degree, the play of personality' (367). In contrast, Maimonides is 'indicating that he will seek to pursue the form of philosophical analysis which contains the least possible theological material. Maimonides prefers to work from philosophical principles which are as pure and logical as possible,

in order to achieve a more satisfactory logical demonstration to religious conclusions.' Leaman, *Moses Maimonides*, 6.

11 Rhees, *Rush Rhees on Religion and Philosophy*, 221.

12 *Ibid.*, 179. Kadushin notes, 'rabbinic thought is not speculative; it is organismic. Rabbinic ideas are not built up by ratiocination; they refer back directly to experience, and hence the integration of thought here is not a matter of design.' Kadushin, *The Rabbinic Mind*, 336.

13 C. H. Dodd, *The Interpretation of the Fourth Gospel* (Cambridge: Cambridge University Press, 1968), 152.

14 *Ibid.* Rhees rightly notes: 'I do not think that Plato's conception of aspiration towards an ideal can be much like the Christian conception of seeking God. Perhaps I can put that by saying that the relation of one's life to God is not the relation of one's life to an ideal.' Rhees, *Rush Rhees on Religion and Philosophy*, 181.

15 Schechter, *Aspects of Rabbinic Theology*, 42.

16 Wittgenstein, *Culture and Value*, 13e.

17 *Ibid.*, 19e.

18 Nevo, 'Religious Belief and Jewish Identity', 226.

19 *Ibid.*, 236.

20 Rhees, 'Postscript', in *Recollections of Wittgenstein*, 177.

21 *Ibid.*

22 *Ibid.*

23 *Ibid.*, 197.

24 Yuval Lurie, 'Jews as a Metaphysical Species', *Philosophy*, 64, 249 (July 1989), 342.

25 *Ibid.*, 325.

26 Gerhard D. Wassermann, 'Wittgenstein on Jews: Some Counter-examples', *Philosophy*, 65 (1990), 355.

27 *Ibid.*

28 *Ibid.*, 365. Ray Monk also discusses Wittgenstein's use of 'the slogans of racist anti-Semitism'. *The Duty of Genius*, 280, 316.

29 David Edmonds and John Eidinow, *Wittgenstein's Poker* (Chatham: Faber & Faber, 2001), 87.

30 *Ibid.*, 90.

31 *Ibid.*, 87.

32 Monk, *The Duty of Genius*, 316–17.

33   *Ibid.*, 314.
34   Wittgenstein, *Culture and Value*, 6e.
35   *Ibid.*, 19e.
36   *Ibid.*, 18e–19e.
37   *Ibid.*, 19e.
38   Wittgenstein, *Wittgenstein's Lectures: 1930–1932*, from the notes of John King and Desmond Lee, ed. Desmond Lee (Chicago: University of Chicago Press, 1989), 26.
39   *Ibid.*, 35.
40   Wittgenstein, *Culture and Value*, 20e.
41   Wittgenstein, *Philosophical Investigations*, § 124.
42   Wittgenstein, *Culture and Value*, 59e–60e.
43   *Ibid.*, 19e.
44   Wittgenstein, *Philosophical Remarks*, Foreword.
45   Wittgenstein, *Culture and Value*, 16e.
46   *Ibid.*, 20e.
47   *Ibid.*, 13e.
48   Plato, *Phaedo*, 66e. In contrast, Abraham Joshua Heschel writes that the 'Bible does not regard the body as the sepulchre and prison house of the soul'. *To Grow in Wisdom: An Anthology of Abraham Joshua Heschel*, ed. Jacob Neusner and Noam M. M. Neusner (New York: Madison Books, 1990), 127.
49   Kadushin, *The Rabbinic Mind*, 336.
50   Berdyaev, *Spirit and Reality*, 15.
51   Rebecca D. Pentz, 'Veatch and Brain Death: A Plea for the Soul', *The Journal of Clinical Ethics*, 5, 2 (Summer 1994), 132. Note too that Calvin regards the idea of the soul as breath to 'err too grossly', bk 1, ch. 15, sec. 2.
52   Pentz, 'Veatch and Brain Death', 133. Nietzsche, in *Beyond Good and Evil*, notes his admiration of the 'Old Testament' in light of its natural embodiment: 'In the Jewish "Old Testament", the book of divine justice, there are human beings, things, and speeches so grand a style that the Greek and Indian literature have nothing to compare with it. With terror and reverence one stands before these tremendous remnants of what man once was' (52).
53   Schechter, *Aspects of Rabbinic Theology*, 144.
54   Pentz, 'Veatch and Brain Death', 133.

55 Plato, *Phaedo*, 66e. Descartes says in the *Discourse* that even if he had no body, he would still be certain of his existence, while on the other hand, if he stopped thinking it would mark the end of his existence. *The Philosophical Writings of Descartes*, 1:127.

56 Job 10:9.

57 Schechter, *Aspects of Rabbinic Theology*, 111. Heschel notes that the 'dichotomy of spirit and letter is alien to Jewish tradition. What man does in his concrete, physical existence is directly relevant to the divine.' Furthermore, the 'Hebrew Bible is not a book about heaven – it is a book about earth.' Abraham Joshua Heschel, *Israel: An Echo of Eternity* (New York: Farrar, Straus & Giroux, 1969), 146.

58 Paul Morris, 'The Embodied Text: Covenant and Torah', *Religion*, 20 (January 1990), 78.

59 In Jeremiah 15:16, God's words are eaten. In reference to Shields, this is certainly bringing the 'sacred' into contact with the 'profane'.

60 Leon Nemoy (ed.), *Yale Judaica Series* (New Haven: Yale University Press, 1959), vol. 8, *The Midrash On Psalms* (*Midrash Tehillim*), vol. 1, trans. William G. Bravde, 32:4.

61 Morris, 'The Embodied Text', 81, 84.

62 *Ibid.*, 78.

63 *Ibid.*

64 Pentz, 'Veatch and Brain Death', 134.

65 This is in contrast to Calvinism, for example, which distances truth from the body and places it squarely in the mind's reasoning, and away from practice.

66 Sacha Stern, *Jewish Identity in Early Rabbinic Writings* (New York: E. J. Brill, 1994), 79.

67 Morris, 'The Embodied Text', 84. Heschel says, 'ontology inquires: what is *being*? What does it mean to be? The religious mind ponders: what is *doing*?' Moreover, 'it would be futile ... to explore the meaning of music and abstain from listening to music. It would be just as futile to explore the Jewish thought from a distance, in self-detachment. Jewish thought is disclosed in Jewish living.' Abraham Joshua Heschel, *Between God and Man: An Interpretation of Judaism*, ed. Fritz A. Rothschild (New York: Harper Brothers, 1959), 81–2.

68   Rhees, *Rush Rhees on Religion and Philosophy*, 12.

69   Gersion Appel, *A Philosophy of Mitzvoth: The Religious-Ethical Concepts of Judaese, Their Roots in Biblical Law and the Oral Tradition* (New York: KTAV Publishing House, 1975), 10.

70   Rhees notes, '(It is not that I praise him *because* he is creator. To say 'Creator' is already praise.) (And already music.)' *Rush Rhees on Religion and Philosophy*, 50.

71   *Ibid.*, 181. Interestingly, we find the base of Shields's method, namely Calvinism, supporting Plato's idea. Calvin believes the purpose of life is the concept of God, 'for it is the very thing which Plato meant when he taught, as he often does, that the chief good of the soul consists in resemblance to God'. Calvin, bk 1, ch. 3, sec. 3. In a sense, this is backward to the Hebraic notion that God becomes like the people in their history and practices.

72   Contrast this with Glenn Gray's estimation of Hegel: 'His God is the God of the philosophers, more Greek than Judaic. Hegel insists that God can be fully known ... through conceptual thought.' J. Glenn Gray, in *G. F. W. Hegel. On Art, Religion, and the History of Philosophy. Introductory Lectures*, ed. J. Glenn Gray (Indianapolis: Hackett, 1997), 19. Moreover, Heschel says, 'if God were a theory, the study of theology would be the way to understand Him. But God is alive and in need of love and worship.' *Between God and Man*, 81.

73   Rhees, *Rush Rhees on Religion and Philosophy*, 313–14.

74   David Stern, *Midrash and Theory* (Evanston, IL: Northwestern University Press, 1996), 91. According to Heschel, 'the Bible tells us nothing about God Himself; all its sayings refer to His relations to man. His own life and essence are neither told nor disclosed.' *Between God and Man*, 111.

75   Schechter, *Aspects of Rabbinic Theology*, 36–7.

76   David Stern, 'Midrash and Indeterminacy', *Critical Inquiry*, 15 (Autumn 1988), 153.

77   Schechter, *Aspects of Rabbinic Theology*, 37.

78   Heschel, *To Grow in Wisdom*, 124.

79   Schechter, *Aspects of Rabbinic Theology*, 33. Stern notes that God and the Hebrews are sometimes even regarded as equals. *Jewish Identity in the Early Rabbinic Writings*, 252.

80   Shields, *Logic and Sin*, 38. It is interesting to note that the Gnostics'
      opposition to the God of the Jews was primarily due to the concrete
      and significant earthy interaction of their God. Robert Grant
      writes, 'it is the feeling of hostility toward the world, toward world-
      accepting Jews, toward the world-creating, sex-creating god of the
      Jews' that separates the speculative Platonism of the Gnostics from
      the Jews' concrete revelation.' *Gnosticism and Early Christianity* (New
      York: Columbia University Press, 1966), 107.

81   Shields, *Logic and Sin*, 31.

82   Heschel, *The Prophets* (New York: Harper & Row, 1962), 232.

83   Heschel, *Between God and Man*, 108.

84   Kadushin, *The Rabbinic Mind*, 280. The first discussions of anthro-
      pomorphism in Jewish thought arose in the Middle Ages due to
      a 'philosophical conception of God predicated upon the absolute
      incorporeality, unity, and incomparability of divine being'. Stern,
      Midrash and Theory, 75.

85   Kadushin, *The Rabbinic Mind*, 287. Heschel writes: 'To the specu-
      lative mind God is the most perfect being, and it is the attribute of
      perfection and its implication of wisdom which serve as a starting
      point for the inquiries into the existence and nature of God. The
      notion of God as a perfect being is not of Biblical extraction. It is
      the product ... of Greek philosophy; a postulate of reason.' *Between
      God and Man*, 97–8.

86   Monk, *The Duty of Genius*, 301.

87   Stern, *Midrash and Theory*, 73.

88   Midrash is derived from the verb *darash* 'to seek, ask', and is
      used particularly within theological connection to God or Torah.
      Basically, 'Midrash cannot be precisely defined, only described',
      and is found in the bible itself as, for example, the books of
      Chronicles being a Midrash on the books of Samuel and Kings.
      Midrash carries on as Rabbinic Midrash; which is not '"objective"
      professional exegesis ... Midrash is primarily a religious activity ...'
      See H. L. Strack and G. Stemberger, *Introduction to the Talmud and
      Midrash*, trans. Markus Bockmuehl (Minneapolis: Fortress Press,
      1992), 255–9.

89   Bruns, *Hermeneutics Ancient and Modern*, 106.

90   *Ibid.*, 113.

91   *Ibid.*, 110.
92   Schechter, *Aspects of Rabbinic Theology*, xxv.
93   Wittgenstein, *Philosophical Investigations*, § 355.
94   Wittgenstein, *Remarks on the Foundations of Mathematics*, ed. G. H. von Wright, Rush Rhees, and G. E. M. Anscombe, trans. G. E. M. Anscombe (Oxford: Basil Blackwell, 1978), 5.
95   Stern, 'Midrash and Indeterminacy', 135.
96   Wittgenstein notes in *Culture and Value* that 'believing means submitting to an authority', 45e.
97   Bruns, *Hermeneutics Ancient and Modern*, 115.
98   *Ibid.*, 113.
99   In the *Midrash on Psalms* (*Midrash Tehillim*), vol. 1, 12:4, the question is raised: 'In what way shall we know the true sense of the law?' God replies: 'The majority is to be followed: When a majority says it is unclean, it is unclean, when a majority says it is clean, it is clean.'
100 Neil Gillman, introduction to Schechter, *Aspects of Rabbinic Theology*, xii.
101 Stern, *Midrash and Theory*, 31.
102 Bruns, *Hermeneutics Ancient and Modern*, 106.
103 Schechter, *Aspects of Rabbinic Theology*, 14.
104 Rhees, *Rush Rhees on Religion and Philosophy*, 99.
105 Stern, *Midrash and Theory*, 12.
106 Wittgenstein, *Philosophical Remarks*, 81.
107 Monk, *The Duty of Genius*, 468.
108 Wittgenstein, *Philosophical Investigations*, § 199, § 202.
109 Peter Ochs, 'Torah, Language and Philosophy: A Jewish Critique', *International Journal for Philosophy of Religion*, 18 (1985), 115.
110 Wittgenstein, *Philosophical Investigations*, § 19.
111 Bruns, *Hermeneutics Ancient and Modern*, 105.
112 Gerald Bruns, 'Midrash and Allegory: The Beginnings of Scriptural Interpretation', in *The Literary Guide to the Bible*, ed. Robert Alter and Frank Kermode (Cambridge: The Belknap Press of Harvard University, 1987), 633.
113 Wittgenstein, *Culture and Value*, 64e.
114 Louis Finkelstein, introduction to *Aspects of Rabbinic Theology*, xviii.
115 Stern, 'Midrash and Indeterminacy', 146, 15.

116   Wittgenstein, *Philosophical Investigations*, p. 226.

117   Exodus 32.

118   Shields, *Logic and Sin*, 76, 84. This argument will be developed in the next section.

119   An idol is understood in this discussion as an external element (e.g. simple object, pre-established conditions, Forms, golden calf, etc.) that is thought to fix meaning and thereby misses the significance of the form of life (history, practices, living, etc.) for meaning.

120   Wittgenstein, 'Sections 86–93 (pp. 405–35) of the so-called "Big Typescript"', 9.

121   Ackermann, *Wittgenstein's City*, 18–19.

122   Shields, *Logic and Sin*, 76.

123   *Ibid.*, 84.

124   *Ibid.*

125   *Ibid.*

126   Calvin, *Institutes of the Christian Religion*, bk 1, ch. 11, sec. 8.

127   Shields, *Logic and Sin*, 76.

128   *Ibid.*, 28–9.

129   Ludwig Wittgenstein, *Remarks on Frazer's Golden Bough*, ed. Rush Rhees, trans. A. C. Miles, revised by Rush Rhees (Atlantic Highlands: Humanities Press International, 1989), 2.

130   Ludwig Wittgenstein, *Lectures and Conversations on Aesthetics, Psychology and Religious Belief*, ed. Cyril Barret (Berkeley: University of California Press), 59.

131   Rhees, *Rush Rhees on Religion and Philosophy*, 70.

132   Wittgenstein, *Lectures and Conversations*, 63.

133   *Ibid.*

134   Exodus 32:4–5. Note that the Israelites have a feast to *Yahweh* (the name of their God before and after the golden calf incident), not some other deity. This shows that the golden calf does not represent a simple rejection of *Yahweh*, but, as will be shown, an object that is condemned.

135   Wittgenstein, *Philosophical Grammar*, 149.

136   James Gustafson, 'Ethics from a Theocentric Perspective', in vol. 1, *Theology and Ethics* (Chicago: University of Chicago Press, 1981), 296.

137 Calvin, *Institutes of the Christian Religion*, bk 1, ch. 11, sec. 4.

138 A calf is not an uncommon image within the Near East (e.g. Apis the Bull in Egypt or the calf shrine at Catal Huyük in Antolia).

139 Heschel, *Between God and Man*, 81–2.

140 Heschel, *Israel: An Echo of Eternity*, 146.

141 Appel, *A Philosophy of Mitzvoth*, 10.

142 Arthur Hertzberg, *Judaism* (New York: George Braziller, 1962), 19.

143 İlham Dilman, *Language and Reality: Modern Perspectives on Wittgenstein* (Belgium: Peeters Publishing House, 1998), 287.

144 Wittgenstein, *Philosophical Grammar*, 66.

145 Wittgenstein, *Culture and Value*, 63e.

146 Wittgenstein, *Philosophical Grammar*, 108.

147 *Ibid.*, 121.

148 Wittgenstein, *Philosophical Investigations*, § 19.

149 Schechter, *Aspects of Rabbinic Theology*, 292.

150 Wittgenstein, *Philosophical Investigations*, § 94.

151 Exodus 20:4.

152 Heschel, *To Grow in Wisdom*, 121–2.

153 In the Buddhist religion, for example, the Buddhists do not think that the statue of the Buddha is the Buddha. However, in Hebraic thought, any religious practice with images is rejected, no matter what degree of representation the object is thought to have.

154 Questions regarding the origins of the calf image in terms of cultural symbols may help us to understand why the image of a calf was used, in contrast to other images, but there is no image that is acceptable for the Israelites to use, and the questions of origins are beyond the scope of this discussion. Yet it is interesting to note that the Egyptians did make use of calf (or bull) images and this may have influenced the Israelites to make a similar object. If this is the case, then the Israelites' use of the golden calf represents the confusion of using a word outside its language-game. The problem with the golden calf is not in and of itself, but that it has no use in the Hebraic form of life and thereby is a confusion.

155 Shields views God as the foundation of Laws – the 'ground of

meaning' – on the analogy of logical form. Shields, *Logic and Sin*, 50–1.

156   This obviously does not mean that the Israelites form of life *is* God; rather, it is a representation of God.

157   Heschel, *To Grow in Wisdom*, 124. Genesis 1:27 reads, 'God created Adam in His own image.' Heschel makes an important point here, namely, 'the image is not in man; it is man' (116).

158   Exodus 19:6.

159   Heschel, *To Grow in Wisdom*, 126.

160   Heschel, *Between God and Man*, 85.

161   Wittgenstein, *The Blue and Brown Books*, 134.

162   *Ibid.*, 27–8.

163   *Ibid.*, 134.

164   Schechter, *Aspects of Rabbinic Theology*, 117. Even God is in a reciprocal relationship with the Israelites: 'He [God] needs us even as we need him' (47).

165   Kadushin, *The Rabbinic Mind*, 356.

166   Gillman, introduction to Schechter, *Aspects of Rabbinic Theology*, xii.

167   Bruns, *Hermeneutics Ancient and Modern*, 113.

168   Wittgenstein, *Philosophical Investigations*, § 199, § 202.

169   Schechter, *Aspects of Rabbinic Theology*, 199.

170   *Ibid.*, 205. The Hebrew term for holy (*qodesh*) in Exodus 19:6 means a thing set apart.

171   Psalm 106: 19–20. Once again, a calf type image is used in the Near East (e.g. Apis the Bull in Egypt or the calf shrine at Catal Huyük in Antolia).

172   Malcolm, *Wittgenstein*, 87–90. Pride is another form of idolatry since it also is contrary to the holiness of God. Thus, the illness within a religious context represents not only idols, but also the imperfect human disposition. Schechter, *Aspects of Rabbinic Theology*, 223.

173   Wittgenstein, *Philosophical Investigations*, § 255.

174   Schechter, *Aspects of Rabbinic Theology*, 273.

175   *Ibid.*, 237.

176   *Ibid.*, 250.

177   *Ibid.*, 83.

178   Wittgenstein, *Philosophical Investigations*, § 111.
179   Wittgenstein, *Culture and Value*, 44e.
180   Wittgenstein, *Philosophical Investigations*, § 92.
181   Heschel, *Between God and Man*, 113.

5

Wittgenstein's Religious Point of View

Hebraic thought is a useful context to discuss the analogy between Wittgenstein's later philosophy and his 'religious point of view'. The cornerstone of this analogy has been Wittgenstein's later conception of language, which must be understood before analogical comparisons of a religious nature can be made. In order to show the distinct nature of Wittgenstein's later philosophy more clearly, and as Wittgenstein himself recommends, his early thought must be addressed.[1]

The atomism of Wittgenstein's Tractarian thought, for example, stipulates that meaning is to be found in the distinction between the complex (the world and composite propositions) and the simple (the simple object and the unified underlying logical syntax). It is thought that if something is complex, then it is possible that it will break down, and then meaning is lost or changed, while the simple object puts a stop to an infinite regression. Shields, as shown in the second chapter, discussed Wittgenstein's thought primarily within a Tractarian context and therefore based his conception of language on the idea that there is a unified foundation external to our concrete practices which functions as an anchor to ensure and explain the meaning of these practices.

Shields not only discusses Wittgenstein's thought as principally Tractarian, he equates his thought with religion. Indeed, he was shown to view Wittgenstein's philosophy as 'fundamentally religious'.[2] He inverted Wittgenstein's remark – theology as grammar[3] – and claimed that we should understand 'grammar as theology, as the study of the will of God'.[4] Thus, Shields reduced Wittgenstein's philosophy to a Tractarian system and finally to religion. In contrast to Shields, I have been arguing that Wittgenstein's writings are not 'fundamentally' religious, and that, if there is to be any dialogue with religion it is certainly not Shields's idea of the Reformed tradition that lends itself to an insightful discussion. Shields's understanding of Wittgenstein's philosophy and 'religious point of view' wrongly identifies a refined Tractarian conception of meaning with Wittgenstein's later position on the subject and identifies it as religious, chooses an inaccurate religious viewpoint, and consequently ends in further confusion rather than clarification.

Malcolm, in contrast to Shields, clarifies the discussion of Wittgenstein's philosophy. Malcolm's initial discussion presents Wittgenstein's philosophy comprehensively, that is, he does not reduce it to a Tractarian conception. Rather, he was shown to discern a change in Wittgenstein's conception of the philosophy of language from early to later. Wittgenstein's later philosophy, for example, moves away from the idea of absolute simples or transcendent foundations to explain meaning for language.[5] Malcolm notes that 'there is no explanation that rises above our language-games, and explains them'.[6] In contrast to theories outside the language-games that attempt to explain meaning, the later Wittgenstein finds meaning in the concrete applications of language. Malcolm's presentation of the distinct nature of Wittgenstein's later thought provided a sound footing from which to discuss an analogical 'religious point of view'.

Malcolm's work is also helpful in that it keeps philosophy and religion distinct. Wittgenstein's philosophy should stand on its own without equating it with religion or atheism. Thus, Malcolm constructively framed the discussion of Wittgenstein's later thought and a 'religious point of view' in analogical terms. The analogy was based on 'Wittgenstein's conception of the grammar of language, and his view of what is paramount in religious life', such as 'an end to explanation'.[7] In particular, however, this study used an aspect of Hebraic thought within the Judaic tradition for discussions of that point of view. The use of Hebraic thought does not question or conflict with Malcolm's analogies. Rather, it more clearly outlines the nature of a specific religious point of view to better illuminate its distinct relationship with Wittgenstein's later philosophy.

Wittgenstein's later thought has been shown to be interested in the simple ('down-to-earth') use of words. It is a mistake to see our actual use of language as a veil behind which the foundation of meaning resides. Wittgenstein writes,

> It is very *remarkable* that we should be inclined to think of civilization – houses, trees, cars, etc. – as separating man from his origins, from what is lofty and eternal, etc. Our civilized environment, along with its trees and plants, strike us then as though it were cheaply wrapped in

cellophane and isolated from everything great, from God, as it were. That is a remarkable picture that intrudes on us.[8]

This aspect of Wittgenstein's later thought – the focus on the concrete and worldly – can be compared favourably to Hebraic thought. Once again, Schechter similarly comments on the problematic tendency to seek transcendent meaning:

> Among the many strange statements by which the Jewish student is struck, when reading modern divinity works, there is none more puzzling to his mind than the assertion of the transcendentalism of the Rabbinic God. Sayings of a fantastic nature, as for instance, ... God's abode ... epithets for God, such as Heaven or Supreme ... or the Master of all Creation [are] Hellenistic phrases which crept into Jewish literature, but never received, in the mouth of a Rabbi, the significance which they had with an Alexandrine philosopher.[9]

The Hebraic God is not accessed through 'metaphysical deductions', but 'through personal experience of his revelation in the world', and as such, 'cannot possibly be removed from it'.[10] For Wittgenstein's later thought and Hebraic thought, any divergence from normative practices to the metaphysical in search of meaning leads to the confusion of taking our viewpoint away from our concrete activities as the mode of meaning (i.e. the language-games and the history and practices of the Israelites) and wrongly directs us to chimeras.

The similarities between Wittgenstein's later thought and Hebraic thought was shown through the example of the Israelites and the golden calf. This example took Wittgenstein's later conception of philosophy and showed its analogical relationship to Hebraic thought. The analogy was based on the serious problem of idols and the 'treatment' for idols. In both Wittgenstein's thought and Hebraic thought, philosophical and religious, idols are to be destroyed since they betray serious confusion.[11] In other words, in the philosophy of language an underlying logical syntax or foundational ideal is a metaphysical construction that may be thought to anchor or explain meaning for language, but is merely a philosophical idol. Once again, Wittgenstein says, 'our illness is this, to want to explain'.[12] Similarly, an object or transcendental theory that is thought to explain or hold the meaning of the Israelite's God is an idol. In Wittgenstein's later thought and within Hebraic thought idols were shown to be serious problems that need 'treatment'.

Wittgenstein's later conception of philosophy was shown to be 'therapeutic' for the problem of philosophical idols by demonstrating that ordinary language reveals meaning in the language-games. Meaning is not explained through metaphysical connections or by positing foundational realms, but is shown in the form of life. In a similar manner, God is not found or explained by a deduction from metaphysical inquiry, presented as a particular object, or a theoretical abstraction in Hebraic thought. Instead, God is shown through the Israelites' history and practices, that is, their form of life. Winch rightly observes that:

> God's reality is certainly independent of what any man may care to think, but what that reality amounts to can only be seen from the religious tradition in which the concept of God is used, and this use is very unlike the use of scientific concepts, say of theoretical entities. ... It is within the religious use of language that the concept of God's reality has a place.[13]

The Hebraic God is known in the practices and theology of the people just as a sense of meaning for language is found in the language-games, neither of which point to an external meaning or foundation beyond normative practices – they show meaning.

The analogy between Wittgenstein's later philosophy and his 'religious point of view' is particularly constructive when discussed in terms of Hebraic thought within the Judaic tradition. They both understand the serious problem of idols comparatively in their respective fields and offer a parallel 'treatment'; namely, to destroy idols and look at the meaning shown by concrete and normative practices in the form of life.

Endnotes

1   Wittgenstein, *Philosophical Investigations*, viii.
2   Shields, *Logic and Sin*, 9.
3   Wittgenstein, *Philosophical Investigations*, § 373.

4 Shields, *Logic and Sin*, 50.

5 Wittgenstein, *Philosophical Investigations*, § 47.

6 *Ibid.*, § 1. Malcolm, *Wittgenstein*, 77–8.

7 *Ibid.*, 92.

8 Wittgenstein, *Culture and Value*, 50e.

9 Schechter, *Aspects of Rabbinic Theology*, 22. It is interesting to note Abraham Heschel's comment that 'Plato planted in the Western mind the consciousness of unseen, eternal ideas, of which the visible world is but a copy. The prophets placed in the Western mind the consciousness of an unseen, eternal God, of whose Will the visible world is a creation.' Heschel, *The Prophets*, 275.

10 Schechter, *Aspects of Rabbinic Theology*, 25.

11 Wittgenstein, 'Sections 86–93 (pp. 405–35) of the so-called "Big Typescript"', 9.

12 Wittgenstein, *Remarks on the Foundations of Mathematics*, 333.

13 Winch, *Ethics and Action*, 12.

Bibliography

Ackermann, Robert John. *Wittgenstein's City*. Amherst, MA: University of Massachusetts Press, 1988.

Appel, Gersion. *A Philosophy of Mitzvoth*: *The Religious-Ethical Concepts of Judaese, Their Roots in Biblical Law and the Oral Tradition*. New York: KTAV Publishing House, 1975.

Augustine, Saint. *Confessions*. Trans. R. S. Pine-Coffin. London: Penguin Books, 1961.

Berdyaev, Nicolas. *Spirit and Reality*. Trans. George Reavey. London: Geoffrey Bles: The Centenary Press, 1939.

Bonhoeffer, Dietrich. *Letters and Papers from Prison*. London: SCM Press, 1971.

Bruns, Gerald. *Hermeneutics Ancient and Modern*. New Haven: Yale University Press, 1992.

—. 'Midrash and Allegory: The Beginnings of Scriptural Interpretation'. In *The Literary Guide to the Bible*, ed. Robert Alter and Frank Kermode. Cambridge: The Belknapp Press of Harvard University, 1987, 625–46.

Canfield, John V. 'Wittgenstein and Zen'. *Philosophy*, 50, 194 (October 1975), 383–408.

Calvin, John. *John Calvin: Institutes of the Christian Religion*. Trans. Henry Beveridge. London: Arnold Hatfield, 1599.

Clack, Brian R. *An Introduction to Wittgenstein's Philosophy of Religion*. Edinburgh: Edinburgh University Press, 1999.

Chomsky, Noam. *Aspects of the Theory of Syntax*. Cambridge, MA: MIT Press, 1965.

DeAngelis, William James. 'Ludwig Wittgenstein – A Religious Point of View? Thoughts on Norman Malcolm's Last Philosophical Project'. *Dialogue*, 36 (Fall 1997), 819–42.

Descartes, Rene. *The Philosophical Writings of Descartes*. Trans. John Cottingham, Robert Stoothoff and Dugald Mudoch. 2 vols. Cambridge: Cambridge University Press, 1985.

—. *The Philosophical Writings of Descartes*. Trans. John Cottingham, Robert Stoothoff, Dugald Murdoch and Anthony Kenny. vol. 3, *The Correspondence*. Cambridge: Cambridge University Press, 1991.

Dilman, İlhman. *Existentialist Critiques of Cartesianism*. London: Macmillan, 1993.

—. *Language and Reality: Modern Perspectives on Wittgenstein*. Belgium: Peeters Publishing House, 1998.

—. *Philosophy and the Philosophic Life*. London, Macmillan, 1992.

—. 'Wittgenstein and the Question of Linguistic Idealism'. (n.p., n.d.).

Dodd, C. H. *The Interpretation of the Fourth Gospel*. Cambridge: Cambridge University Press, 1968.

Doestoevsky, Fyodor. *The Brothers Karamazov*. Trans. Ralph E. Matlan. New York: W. W. Norton, 1976.

Drury, M. O'C. *The Danger of Words and Writings on Wittgenstein*. Ed. David Berman, Michael Fitzgerald and John Hayes. Bristol: Thoemmes Press, 1996.

—. 'Conversations with Wittgenstein', in *Recollections of Wittgenstein*. Ed. Rush Rhees, 97–171. Oxford: Oxford University Press, 1984.

—. 'Some Notes on Conversations with Wittgenstein', in *Recollections of Wittgenstein*. Ed. Rush Rhees, 76–96. Oxford: Oxford University Press, 1984.

Edmonds, David and John Eidinow. *Wittgenstein's Poker*. Chatham: Faber & Faber, 2001.

Engelmann, Paul. *Letters From Ludwig Wittgenstein, with a Memoir*. Ed. B. F. McGuinness. Trans. L. Furtmüller. Oxford: Basil Blackwell, 1967.

Finkelstein, Louis. Introduction to *Aspects of Rabbinic Theology*, by Solomon Schechter. Woodstock, VT: Jewish Lights Publishing, 1993.

Fischel, Henry A. 'The Transformation of Wisdom in the World of Midrash'. In *Aspects of Wisdom in Judaism and Early Christianity*. Ed. Robert L. Wilken. London: University of Notre Dame Press, 1975.

Fodor, Jerry. *The Language of Thought*. Hassocks, Sussex: Harvester Press, 1975.

Gillman, Neil. Introduction to *Aspects of Rabbinic Theology*, by Solomon Schechter. Woodstock, VT: Jewish Lights Publishing, 1993.

Grant, Robert. *Gnosticism and Early Christianity*. New York: Columbia University Press, 1966.

Gray, Glenn J., ed. In *G. F. W. Hegel. On Art, Religion, and the History of Philosophy. Introductory Lectures.* Indianapolis: Hackett, 1997.

Greer, Rowan A. 'Introduction' in *Origen.* Trans. and Intro. by Rowan A. Greer, 1–37. Mahwah, NJ: Paulist Press, 1979.

Gustafson, James. 'Ethics from a Theocentric Perspective'. Vol. 1, *Theology and Ethics.* Chicago: University of Chicago Press, 1981.

Hertzberg, Arthur. *Judaism.* New York: George Braziller, 1962.

Heschel, Abraham Joshua. *Between God and Man: An Interpretation of Judaism.* New York: Harper Brothers, 1959.

—. *Israel: An Echo of Eternity.* New York: Farrar, Straus & Giroux, 1969.

—. *The Prophets.* New York: Harper & Row, 1962.

—. *To Grow in Wisdom: An Anthology of Abraham Joshua Heschel.* Ed. Jacob Neusner and Noam M. M. Neusner. New York: Madison Books, 1990.

Ibn Gabirol, Solomon. *The Fountain of Life.* New York: Philosophical Library, 1962.

Kerr, Fergus. Review of *Logic and Sin in the Writings of Ludwig Wittgenstein,* by Phillip R. Shields. In *Modern Theology,* 10 (July 1994), 299–301.

—. *Theology After Wittgenstein.* Oxford: Basil Blackwell, 1986.

Kadushin, Max. *The Rabbinic Mind.* New York: Bloch, 1972.

Lawrence, D. H. *The Letters of D. H. Lawrence,* vol. 1, ed. J. T. Boulton. Cambridge: Cambridge University Press, 1979.

Leaman, Oliver. *Moses Maimonides.* New York: Routledge, 1990.

Levi, Albert. 'The Biographical Sources of Wittgenstein's Ethic'. *Telos,* 38 (Winter 1979), 63–76.

Lurie, Yuval. 'Jews as a Metaphysical Species'. *Philosophy,* 64, 249 (July 1989), 323–47.

Lyas, Colin. *Peter Winch.* Teddington: Acumen, 1999.

Maimonides, Moses. *The Guide for the Perplexed.* Trans. M. Friedländer. New York: Dover Publications, 1961.

Malcolm, Norman. *Wittgenstein: A Religious Point of View?* Ed. Peter Winch. New York: Cornell University Press, 1995.

Monk, Ray. *Ludwig Wittgenstein: The Duty of Genius.* London: Jonathan Cape, 1990.

Morris, Paul. 'The Embodied Text: Covenant and Torah'. *Religion,* 20 (January 1990), 77–87.

Nemoy, Leon, ed. *Yale Judaica Series.* Vol. 8, *The Midrash On Psalms*

(*Midrash Tehillim*), vols 1 and 2, trans. William G. Bravde. New Haven: Yale University Press, 1959.

Nevo, Isaac. 'Religious Belief and Jewish Identity in Wittgenstein's Philosophy'. *Philosophy Research Archives*, 13 (1987–88), 225–43.

Nietzsche, Friedrich. *Beyond Good and Evil.* Trans. Helen Zimmern and Walter Kaufmann. New York: Vintage Books, 1966.

—. *Twilight of the Idols.* Trans. R. J. Hollingdale. Harmondsworth: Penguin, 1968.

Ochs, Peter. 'Torah, Language and Philosophy: A Jewish Critique'. *International Journal for Philosophy of Religion*, 18 (1985), 115–22.

Origen. *De Principiis*, in *The Ante-Nicene Fathers.* Ed. Alexander Roberts and James Donaldson, vol. 4. Buffalo: Christian Literature Publishing Company, 1887.

Pentz, Rebecca D. 'Veatch and Brain Death: A Plea for the Soul'. *The Journal of Clinical Ethics*, 5:2 (Summer 1994), 132–5.

Pettersen, Alvyn. *Athanasius and the Human Body.* Bristol: Bristol Press, 1990.

Phillips, D. Z. *Wittgenstein and Religion.* London: Macmillan, 1993.

Plato. *Meno.* Trans. G. M. A. Grube. Indianapolis: Hackett Publishing, 1977.

—. *Phaedo.* Trans. G. M. A. Grube. Indianapolis: Hackett Publishing, 1977.

—. *The Republic of Plato.* Trans. Francis MacDonald Cornford. London: Oxford University Press, 1958.

Rhees, Rush, ed. *Discussions of Wittgenstein.* Bristol: Thoemmes Press, 1996.

—, ed. *Recollections of Wittgenstein.* Oxford: Oxford University Press, 1984.

—. *Rush Rhees on Religion and Philosophy.* Ed. D. Z. Phillips and Mario von der Ruhr. Cambridge: Cambridge University Press, 1997.

—. *Wittgenstein and the Possibility of Discourse.* Ed. D. Z. Phillips. Cambridge: Cambridge University Press, 1998.

Roberts, Alexander and James Donaldson. *Ante-Nicene Fathers.* Translations of the Writings of the Fathers down to A.D. 325. Vol. 4. Buffalo: The Christian Literature Publishing Company, 1887.

Schechter, Solomon. *Aspects of Rabbinic Theology*, with introductions by Neil Gillman and Louis Finkelstein. Woodstock, VT: Jewish Lights Publishing, 1993.

Shields, Philip R. *Logic and Sin in the Writings of Ludwig Wittgenstein.* London: University of Chicago Press, 1993.

Slattery, Denis Patrick. 'Corrupting Corpse vs. Reasoned Abstraction: The Play of Evil in The Brothers Karamazov'. *Dostoevsky Studies*, 1, 1 (1993), 3–23.

Springsted, Eric O. Review of *Logic and Sin in the Writings of Ludwig Wittgenstein*, by Phillip R. Shields. In *Cross Currents*, 43, 3 (Fall 1993), 411–13.

Stern, David. *Midrash and Theory.* Evanston, IL: Northwestern University Press, 1996.

—. 'Midrash and Indeterminacy'. *Critical Inquiry*, 15 (1988), 133–61.

Stern, Sacha. *Jewish Identity in Early Rabbinic Writings.* New York: E. J. Brill, 1994.

Strack, H. L. and G. Stemberger. *Introduction to the Talmud and Midrash*, with a foreword by Jacob Neusner. Trans. Markus Bockmuehl. Minneapolis: Fortress Press, 1992.

Tilgham, B. R. 'Isn't Belief in God an Attitude?', *Philosophy of Religion*, 43, 1 (February 1998), 17–28.

Ullendorff, Edward. 'Thought Categories in the Hebrew Bible', in *Rationalism Judaism and Universalism*. Ed. Raphael Loewe, 273–88. London: Routledge & Kegan Paul, 1966.

Wassermann, Gerhard D. 'Wittgenstein on Jews: Some Counter-examples'. *Philosophy*, 65 (1990), 355–65.

Winch, Peter. 'Discussion of Malcolm's Essay', in *Wittgenstein: A Religious Point of View?* Ed. Peter Winch, 95–135. New York: Cornell University Press, 1995.

—. *Ethics and Action.* London: Routledge & Kegan Paul, 1972.

—. 'Judgement: Propositions and Practices'. *Philosophical Investigations*, 21, 3 (July 1998), 189–202.

—. *The Idea of a Social Science.* London: Routledge & Kegan Paul, 1958.

—. *Trying to Make Sense.* Oxford: Basil Blackwell, 1987.

Wittgenstein, Ludwig. *Culture and Value.* Ed. G. H. von Wright in collaboration with Heikki Nyman. Trans. Peter Winch. Chicago: University of Chicago Press, 1984.

—. *Wittgenstein's Lectures, 1930–32. From the Notes of John King and Desmond Lee.* Ed. Desmond Lee. Chicago: University of Chicago Press, 1989.

—. *Wittgenstein's Lectures, 1932–35. From the Notes of Alice Ambrose and Margaret*

MacDonald. Ed. Alice Ambrose. Chicago: University of Chicago Press, 1989.

—. *Lectures and Conversations on Aesthetics, Psychology and Religious Belief.* Ed. Cyril Barret. Berkeley: University of California Press.

—. 'Lecture on Ethics'. *Philosophical Review*, 74 (January 1965), 3–12.

—. 'Letters to von Wright', in *The Cambridge Review*, 28 February, 1983.

—. *Notebooks*. Ed. G. H. von Wright and G. E. M. Anscombe. Trans. G. E. M. Anscombe. Oxford: Blackwell, 1979.

—. *On Certainty*. Ed. G. E. M. Anscombe and G. H. von Wright. Trans. Denis Paul and G. E. M. Anscombe. Oxford: Basil Blackwell, 1979.

—. *Philosophical Grammar*. Ed. Rush Rhees. Trans. A. J. P. Kenny. Oxford: Blackwell, 1974.

—. *Philosophical Investigations*. Trans. G. E. M. Anscombe. Oxford: Basil Blackwell, 1988.

—. *Philosophical Remarks*. Ed. Rush Rhees. Trans. Raymond Hargreaves and Roger White. Oxford: Basil Blackwell, 1975.

—. *Remarks on Frazer's Golden Bough*. Ed. Rush Rhees. Trans. A. C. Miles, revised by Rush Rhees. Atlantic Highlands: Humanities Press International, 1989.

—. *Remarks on the Foundations of Mathematics*. Ed. G. H. von Wright, Rush Rhees, G. E. M. Anscombe. Trans. G. E. M. Anscombe. Oxford: Basil Blackwell, 1978.

—. *The Blue and Brown Books*. Oxford: Basil Blackwell, 1972.

—. *The so-called Diktat Für Schlick*. Approx. 1931–33.

—. *Tractatus Logico-Philosophicus*. Trans. C. K. Ogden. London: Routledge & Kegan Paul, 1986.

—. 'Sections 86–93 (pp. 405–35) of the so-called "Big Typescript"'. Ed. Heikki Nyman. Trans. C. G. Luckhardt and M. A. E. Aue. *Synthese*, 87, 1 (April 1991), 3–22.

—. *Zettel*. Ed. G. E. M. Anscombe and G. H. von Wright. Trans. G. E. M. Anscombe. Oxford: Blackwell, 1967.

—. *Wittgenstein and the Vienna Circle*. Conversations recorded by Friedrich Waismann. Ed. Brian McGuinness. Trans. Joachim Schulte and Brian McGuinness. Oxford: Basil Blackwell, 1979.

Index